W. Mark Wallis

A PROFOUND CONTRADICTION

A Racial Autobiography

For my best friend, wife of 50 years, and partner in the Faith

Susan Setliff Wallis

and

Brett Wiley, Anna Kate Wiley, and Taylor Byrne

Acknowledgements

Thanks to my daughter Amy Wiley for reading, critiquing, and editing this manuscript during a very busy time of her life.

And thanks to Mabel Lee Mackoy who traveled to Lynchburg, Virginia, in 1931 to do valuable genealogical research and for her research of the history of Greenup County, Kentucky.

A Profound Contradiction

A Racial Autobiography

©2024 W. Mark Wallis

print ISBN: 979-8-35094-159-3

ebook ISBN: 979-8-35094-160-9

Contents

Introduction

"To learn history is to learn context... You may be oblivious to the racial traumas you are carrying or the prejudices you harbor. Writing a racial autobiography is one way to uncover formative experiences around race and deliberately glean lessons and insights from those experiences. A racial autobiography is a self-reported account of your history with race, and its purpose is twofold: to better understand your own story and to build empathy for others.

"We need to study history not simply to know more about the past but to know more about ourselves. History is about identity. Rightly remembering our communal stories is a way of situating ourselves within a broader narrative. History tells us who and where we come from, how the people and events before us have shaped who we are now, and what kind of actions we need to take in order to pursue a more racially just future. Without a sense of history we lose our sense of self."

Jemar Tisby, "How to Study the History of Race"

The past few years I've been researching my family history and building a family tree on Ancestry.com. I grew up hearing I was a descendant of Texas pioneers and was a "true Texan." I was born in 1950, and my hometown, Richardson, Texas, had a population of 1,000 people that year. I am a third-generation graduate of Richardson High School in 1968—and my graduating class was around 1,000 students. A lot of change happened during that time.

In addition, I grew up with a general narrative that my ancestors were "church" people, but not just any church people. We were members of the Church of Christ, and my heritage in that movement went back to the early 1800's. So, there were two general storylines I grew up with:

- Sixth-generation Texan and a descendant of Dallas County Pioneers
- Seventh-generation member of the Church of Christ

My search was casual until the events of 2020 and the period of the pandemic. In the fall of 2020, my wife Susan and I participated in an online small-group Bible study via Zoom, led by some friends at the Southwest Church of Christ in Amarillo, Texas. The study was based on *The Color of Compromise Video Study* by Jamar Tisby (available on Amazon Prime). That study was eye-opening and encouraged me to be more proactive in examining my racial history. I believed that I was in a unique position to look back on my family history and experience to shed light on the racial injustices that existed in this country. I felt it was time to come to grips with my own blind spots and prejudices—especially as it related to how my church and family's record on race had been hidden and sanitized.

So, in 2021, I engaged some professional researchers at Ancestry.com to research some of the history around my third great grandfather (on my dad's side of the family), John B. Floyd. I wanted to learn about his role in founding the Richardson Church of Christ and his involvement with the Church of Christ in Kentucky. In addition, he was known to have brought enslaved people to Texas from Kentucky. The family narrative I heard was that John B. Floyd brought enslaved people from Kentucky, but they were "happy slaves" and even stayed with his family after they were given their freedom. So, I asked the researchers to see if they could find out if he did indeed have slaves and how they eventually were granted their freedom. Some very enlightening and historically important facts were uncovered during the months of the research project.

In 2022, I engaged Ancestry.com to research the history of Moses Mackoy, my third great grandfather (on my mother's side of the family), who lived in Greenup, Kentucky. He was a minister and founded the Siloam Christian Church and the Greenup Christian church in Kentucky. He taught at a literacy school for slaves around 1817, and his father had many slaves. I wanted to learn more about his role as a church minister and more about the family history of owning slaves. This research also was very enlightening.

America lives by myths that do not match up with history. The Bible does not sugarcoat history. It tells the good, the bad, and the ugly. Christians are instructed to confess their sins to one another. As Christians, we should look at well-attested historical information and learn from it. I have never learned much of anything by simply staring at a statue. It has no context. When you tour the British Museum, the Vatican, the Louvre, the Uffizi Gallery, etc.—you don't learn much just looking at the statues or paintings. You need a trained academic guide to explain the context of the painting or statue to help you understand what it means.

> *"Many Christians supported slavery to the extent that they were willing to risk their lives to protect it, has not been fully considered in the American church, even though 150 years have passed since the war. Slavery has always been a profound contradiction at the heart of both the United States and the American church."*

> *Jemar Tisby,* The Color of Compromise

So, this book is an attempt at a partial autobiography dealing with family history, church history, and the history of race in America. The trail of my family's history surprisingly led all the way back to the year 1619.

Some of this history will only meet the standard of family lore as I heard it. I acknowledge other family members may remember different versions or variants of the oral history. I have simply recounted how I remember these stories, since those memories specifically impacted the formation of who I am. However, I found a significant amount of written history in books, family records, newspapers, and census records.

This journey talks about people of faith who did a lot of brave things and helped build this country. But they also had significant and damaging "blind spots." I wonder what my blind spots are. I hope from this book that my descendants at least know that I was willing to try and better understand my identity.

It is a story with profound contradictions. Let's begin with the "Jesus Prayer."

"Lord Jesus, Son of God, have mercy upon me, a sinner."

TIMELINE

1619— Dr. John Woodson arrives in Virginia

1705— The Virginia Commonwealth legal code declares slavery of Black and indigenous people

1801— Lavina and John Mackoy move from Virginia to Greenup, Kentucky

1817— Moses Fuqua Mackoy starts literacy school for enslaved people in Greenup, KY

1831— Stone-Campbell church movement formally begins in Kentucky

1835— Siloam church in Greenup, KY becomes a Church of Christ

1836— Texas becomes an independent Republic and legalizes slavery

1855— John B. Floyd moves from Kentucky to North Texas

1860— "Political Meeting" held in Dallas chaired by John B. Floyd

1860— City of Dallas is destroyed by fire

1861-1865— The Civil War

1874— Richardson Church of Christ established by John Floyd, James Floyd, and Joseph Broad

1876— John L. Mackoy moves to North Texas

1870-1964— The Jim Crow Era

1890— The proliferation of Confederate monuments begins

1916— City of Dallas Charter amended to provide for racial segregation of housing

1930— Patsy Ruth Mackoy is born

1930— The Sherman, Texas Riot

1931— Mabel Lee Mackoy travels to Lynchburg, VA to study genealogy of Mackoy family

1950— Bombing of Black owned homes in South Dallas

1950— W. Mark Wallis is born

1957— Majority of faculty and students of Harding College sign statement advocating integration of the school

1963— The assassination of President John Kennedy

1968— Assassination of Martin Luther King

1969— Black students at Harding College walk out of chapel service in protest

1970— Richardson Independent School District is integrated

1972— Dallas Cowboys football team wins Super Bowl VI

1974— Susan and Mark Wallis are married in Dallas

1978— The TV show, "Dallas" is first aired

1979— The TV show, "The Dukes of Hazard" is first aired

1980— Elsie Faye Higgins, Black community organizer, is elected to the Dallas City Council

2001— Susan and Mark Wallis move to Denver, Colorado

2018— National Lynching Memorial opened in Montgomery, Alabama

2018— Botham Jean murdered in his apartment by Dallas police officer

2020— Death of George Floyd and Black Lives Matter protests

2021— Texas Legislature places restrictions on social studies curriculum in public schools

Chapter 1

STAGECOACH INN

The Floyd Inn—rendering by unknown artist from 1999 Memorial dedication invitation

I grew up with a strong historical connection to Dallas and more specifically to my deep roots in the neighboring city of Richardson. My mother was just 19 and my father 22 when I was born at St. Paul Hospital in Dallas, Texas, on November 19, 1950. We lived in Richardson with my grandparents in the same house where my dad was born on Greenville Avenue. The little home with white siding sat near a huge pecan tree, and about a mile south of the Floyd Pioneer Cemetery where my third great-grandfather, John B. Floyd, purchased 900 acres of land in 1855. It was once the small town of Breckenridge. Today it's home to Texas Instruments and Restland Cemetery. I was raised to know my ancestors were Floyds and that this carried some weight. In 1955, my parents built a modest home directly behind my grandparents' house. I lived there until I left for Harding College in the fall of 1968.

Our home was within walking distance of Richardson High School, and more importantly, the football stadium. Texas football creates an energy you won't find across state lines, and the so-called Friday night lights are a draw to all ages. My dad dutifully took me and my brother to all the home games and even some away games. I loved it. I sat in the stands amongst the roaring crowd and dreamed of one day suiting up to play for the Eagles myself.

Unfortunately, the intensity that comes with football in the Lone Star State also means one's athletic fate can be decided at an excruciatingly young age. I still remember the first week of seventh grade and the imposing football coach in the hallway with a clipboard bearing the names of boys who were chosen to go out for the team. To my great disappointment, my name was not on the list.

My plan for playing for the Eagles ended that day, and I did not know what I was going to do. The band seemed like my next best option, and that choice became available to me in the eighth grade. The junior high band director was Robert Floyd. I came to learn we were distant cousins. He took an interest in me and steered me toward the coronet. The Golden Eagle band was one of the top bands in Texas, and spots were coveted and hard-earned. It looked like I would be headed for the second-string Cadet Band, but Director Floyd switched me to trumpet in ninth grade, knowing there would be an opening. He went to bat for me, and I made the Golden Eagle band my sophomore year. I ended up following in the footsteps of my grandfather, Clint Wallis. He played trumpet and traveled with the Richardson Community Band to Washington, D.C., to perform at the inauguration of President Woodrow Wilson. This was the first time I experienced a tangible benefit to being related to the Floyds.

John B. Floyd was born on April 29, 1808, in Kentucky and married Julia Ann Lindsay in Gallatin on October 14, 1833. He began a career as a state legislator around 1830 and by that time was living in Trimble County, Kentucky. He served for two terms and attended the 1830 and 1832 Jackson Conventions.

My research on John B. Floyd revealed a draw to the wide-open spaces of Texas that led him to make the long journey from Kentucky. He bought a horse along the way and rode it until he reached Dallas. He bought 900 acres of land for $4.00 per acre, then returned to Kentucky. He eventually returned with his wife and six children to a pole shack cabin and started working on the place. The result was the first two-story house in Dallas County.

The home became an inn offering lodging to weary travelers making the long trips between settlements. Its highly traveled location drew notable guests to the inn. Family stories note that Sam Bass and Belle Starr were frequent guests. One of the more colorful tales includes dinner table talk about the Younger brothers, who were famous outlaws at the time.

> *"Grandma Floyd was serving and said, 'Just let them Younger brothers come around here and I'll show them the way to go!' A handsome young man rose from the table and politely said, "Madam, I'm Cole Younger." There was no recorded response to this electric moment, but possibly she countered, 'Have another biscuit?' It has also been told that because of the good cover, the James gang and the Younger brothers used the 'Old Thicket' to hide their horses. Rumor has it that there may still be buried treasure there."*[1]

Another outlaw met his fate when officers shot him in front of the inn. He's buried at Restland in the Floyd Family Cemetery.

Tales like this are legendary in Texas. From a young age, I was fed the notion that Texas is bigger and better than any other state, and it was a blessing to be a Southerner. Thankfully, we had the good fortune to avoid being born "Yankees." I also grew up with the distinction of being a sixth-generation Texan who was a descendant of brave pioneers who were well known in Dallas County.

John B. Floyd was also a Christian who helped found the Church of Christ in Richardson. My family considered this the most important thing he did. He came from Kentucky and was part of the "Stone-Campbell" church movement that formally began in Lexington, Kentucky, on December 31, 1831. This group sought to "restore" the church back to its original form and to just be Christians.

The family lore also included that the Floyds owned slaves. This is confirmed by historical records. There were certainly slaves in the Richardson area. Probably some of the first feet to touch the ground as the settlers arrived from the east were those of the slaves helping women and children from the covered wagons. Written records show that there were slaves with the Jacksons, Floyds, and Campbells. However, unlike others, they were said to be benevolent slaveowners. Their slaves "gladly" made the trip from Kentucky to Texas because they had such "good lives." The story goes that the enslaved people enjoyed this arrangement so much they stuck around with the family after the Civil War. "They were happy slaves." This was the "myth" that in my relatives' minds avoided what was and is "a profound contradiction."

Chapter 2

SHOTGUN

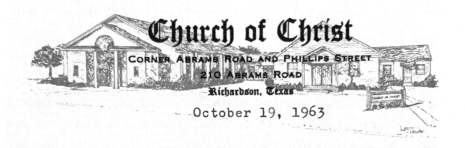

Church of Christ
CORNER ABRAMS ROAD AND PHILLIPS STREET
210 ABRAMS ROAD
Richardson, Texas
October 19, 1963

My great-aunt, Alice Saunders, was sitting on the front porch of the Abrams Road Church of Christ one afternoon, probably around 1900. James L. Floyd stood on that church porch next to her, holding a shotgun.

Alice was the older sister of my grandmother, Winnie Lee Saunders (Granny), who was born in Richardson, Texas, in 1896. Her father, Thomas B. Saunders, was a farmer and formerly a Scout in the Confederate army. He married Annie A. Floyd, who was the daughter of James L. Floyd and Alice Broad. As a kid I was always told that Granny was a Floyd and that the Floyds were a well-known pioneer family. Floyd Road, which runs north/south from LBJ Freeway to Waterview Rd. in Richardson was named after them. Thomas Saunders died at the age of 40 from complications from a farming accident. Granny told of how they amputated his leg in the kitchen of their house which resulted in an infection that took his life. Life was hard around the turn of the 20th century.

Standing next to Alice Saunders on that church porch was James Lindsay Floyd, aka "Daddy Floyd." James was a founding trustee of the Abrams Road Church of Christ along with his father John B. Floyd and his father-in-law Joseph Broad.

The Abrams Road Church of Christ was officially formed in 1874, one year after the city of Richardson, Texas, was founded. The congregation had a two-cup silver communion set that was given to John B. Floyd by the Church of Christ in Trimble, Kentucky. I guess for a while they were "two-cuppers." (That is an inside joke for those of you who grew up in the Church of Christ.) John B. Floyd gave the two acres of land at Abrams Road and Phillips Street, and a church building was erected on the site. The original building was badly damaged by a tornado in 1909 and was destroyed by fire in 1917. Following the fire, the church did not formally reorganize until 1939, at which time they began to meet in the Vickery Community House. My Granny, Winnie Saunders Wallis, was a key person who held this small church together during this time of transition. In 1943, a new building was erected on the original lot. I remember this building from when I was probably about five years old. It was a small building with a large stone exterior and the "auditorium" had a baptistry behind the pulpit with a mural on the wall depicting a winding river—maybe intended to be the Jordan River. I don't think it was air-conditioned because I remember members waving hand fans during the sermon. Richardson was growing dramatically with the addition of Collins Radio and Texas Instruments. The town took on the nickname of "The Electronic City." In 1956, a new air-conditioned auditorium was added to the site. The congregation had difficulties with the contractor who was constructing the auditorium, so the members had to pitch in and do a lot of finishing work. I remember going with my dad on a Saturday to work on the building, and he gave me a small putty knife for me to use. I was baptized by Johnny Jackson in that church building on October 16, 1963. I also remember the time I decided to sit in the balcony for Sunday morning worship, but that plan ended abruptly when my dad walked up behind me and thumped me on the head and told me to get downstairs where I belonged. The Abrams Road church planted the Waterview Church of Christ on the west side of Richardson in 1962. In 1967, the Abrams Road church moved to a new location on South Plano Road and changed its name to the Richardson East Church of Christ.

My grandfather, William Clinton (Clint) Wallis ("Daddy Clint"), was an elder in the Abrams Road Church of Christ before I was born. He never resigned as an elder even after he went to live in the Christian Care Center nursing home. The church eventually gave him the title of "Elder Emeritus." He was not always a member of the Church of Christ. His father, Rev. William Clinton Wallis, Sr., was the pastor of the First Methodist Church of Richardson, founded in 1886. He was pastor of that church until November 1911 when he was struck by a train while riding in a cotton wagon in Richardson, Texas. Rev. William Wallis had been a physically abusive father to Clint and even refused to let his wife attend church so that she could instead prepare lunch. The Wallis family farm was located near Beltline Road and Waterview Drive, and the original farmhouse remains there today. When Clint married my Grandmother Winnie, he was a dedicated member of the Methodist church, so he faithfully attended the Methodist church while Winnie and their children attended the Church of Christ. When the Methodist church had a "meal on the grounds," Winnie would prepare food for Clint to take. Clint became a member of the Abrams Road Church of Christ after his middle daughter Mildred decided to be baptized. Mildred had some mental and physical disabilities that made her life challenging, but she came to the conviction she wanted to be baptized. Clint said that if she has decided to be baptized, then he needed to also be baptized. (I assume he had been baptized as an infant.) Clint was well-known in the small town of Richardson and was referred to as the "most honest man in town." He managed the Huguley Cotton Gin in Richardson for several years until it was sold in 1934. So, he hired many people in the community, including Black men. He was out of work during this time of the Depression, and he did some farming and had a small dairy business that provided milk to homes in the community. This was a difficult time; they were sometimes what we would today call "food insecure," and he was unable to make mortgage payments on the house. A couple of years later, the postmaster job in Richardson became available, a position traditionally appointed by the State Senator. However, three people applied for the position, including Clint. The Senator did not want to take sides, so he decided there would be an election held to determine who would become postmaster. A few members of the Black community told Clint that if they were allowed to vote he would get their votes. However, if you were Black in Richardson, Texas, in 1936, poll taxes and other registration laws prevented Black people from voting in general elections. However, Clint narrowly won the election, served as postmaster for 21 years and continued to work in the post office for another seven years after he retired. In addition, Clint was a member of the Richardson Rotary Club and served some time as president. He never missed a meeting, including when he was out of town. I distinctly remember him taking me to a meeting when I was in high school, and I saw how he was a respected member of the community. When Clint became a member of the Abrams Road Church of Christ, he was asked to become an elder almost immediately.

I grew up in a small house that was directly behind the house at 704 Greenville Avenue where my grandparents lived. This was the location of the family dairy farm they ran during the Depression. I walked through their yard on the way to school every day. I remember their house was cool (thanks to air conditioning), and Granny always had a supply of cold king-sized Cokes to drink. They had a significant influence on my life just by their presence, and I never wanted to disappoint them. They had both lost their fathers to tragedy when they were young and had lost their daughter, Mildred, when she was only 22 years old. Winnie and Clint were resilient people that were vibrant and active until the last couple of years of their lives.

So, why was my great-great grandfather, James Lindsay Floyd, standing on the front porch of the Abrams Road Church of Christ one afternoon near the beginning of the 20th century? A certain group of members were bringing a piano to be placed in the church sanctuary. Their attempt was rebuffed. "The Church," the true church, only sang a capella.

Around 1985, the Richardson East Church of Christ sold its building on South Plano Road to Furr's Cafeteria for a very good price. The building built 20 years earlier had a cavernous sanctuary that was not ideal and maintenance issues had been problems for years. A new building site was acquired on east Campbell Road, but it would be some time before that building would be complete. So, the First Christian Church offered to let the Richardson East Church meet in their building while their new building was under construction. Christian churches and the Churches of Christ had previously split over the use of musical instruments in worship at around the turn of the 20th century. The Richardson East Church had a town hall meeting on a Sunday afternoon to discuss logistics and other matters related to the temporary arrangement to meet in the First Christian building. Larry James, Sr., Minister of the Richardson East group, conducted the meeting, then asked if anyone had any comments or questions. To Larry's surprise, 90-year-old Clint Wallis raised his hand and stood up to make a comment. Larry had no idea what he was going to say. Clint said that everyone should be very grateful for First Christian graciously allowing the use of their sanctuary. And he added that he did not ever want to hear a Richardson East church member ever making critical and/or judgmental comments regarding the First Christian Church. He sat down.

Clint was unarmed.

Chapter 3

THE REAL MACKOYS

SILOAM CHURCH OF CHRIST, 1954
WALTER MACKOY AND RUTH MACKOY

My maternal grandfather, Walter Price Mackoy, was born on December 31, 1908, in Ellis County, Texas, along with his twin brother, Robert. Walter was a true Texan, but in a humble way. Being in his presence, it was clear this wasn't his "first rodeo." Walter married Mary Cleo Crumbie on October 12, 1929, when he was 20 years old. They had two daughters, my mother Patsy

Ruth and Margaret Faye. Walter was a farmer, rancher, fisherman, and hunted quail with a single shot shotgun while holding two shells in the fingers of his left hand so that he could rapidly reload. Walter was also the most sincerely reverent man I have ever been around. He was a serious Christian who always had his well-worn Bible on the table in the den of their home. You could just feel his spirituality when you were around him. He had a good sense of humor and was young enough to throw a baseball around with me and my brother when we were kids. He played a bit of golf in his later years and even had a golf cup hole in his backyard for a while. He always had a Ford pickup (with zero options) that he would let my brother and me drive around on the farm as soon as we could reach the pedals. We would ride in the truck bed when he drove out to their farm, which was three miles from Whitesboro, Texas. He would always honk the horn as the truck entered the tunnel that went below the railroad track on the edge of town. I also remember riding on the axle of the tractor while he was plowing the fields. Yes, that was probably not the wisest thing to do, but you did learn to how to focus at a young age.

Walter's dad was Samuel Walter Mackoy, and he was born in Greenup County, Kentucky, in 1871. Samuel's father, John Lawson Mackoy, moved his family from Kentucky to Ellis, Texas, in January of 1876. They were farmers in Ellis County, Texas, and Samuel later moved to Quannah, Texas, and then to Grayson County, Texas. In his later years, Sam Mackoy went to live with Walter and Cleo on their farm outside of Whitesboro, Texas. My mother, Pat, really loved Sam; she remembered him being funny and making her feel special. She also remembered how he would be overcome with worry when bad weather started rolling in over the farm. He would pace back and forth on the front porch worrying that the crops in the field might be ruined or that a tornado might hit the barn or house. Sam had experienced tragedy in his life. His wife, Mary Margaret Vines, died at age 37 from pneumonia and left him with five children under the age of eight. His son Robert died at nine years of age from an infection in his leg, and his first daughter, Florence, committed suicide at age 39. He lived through the first pandemic, World Wars I and II, and lived on the edge of poverty during the Great Depression. His generation lived through some difficult times, and it seems appropriate that he would be pacing on that front porch. He knew that life could deal you a blow at any moment.

Samuel Mackoy was the son of John Lawson Mackoy and Mary Eliza Mackoy. John Lawson Mackoy was born in 1831 in Greenup, Kentucky. His family Bible records the story of him moving his family to Ellis County, Texas, in January of 1876. He was known as a prominent farmer in the county until he died in November of 1897.

When I talk about my Mackoy ancestors, I am usually asked if they were involved in the infamous "Hatfield-McCoy feud." The feuding McCoys of Kentucky were descendants of a William McCoy. My family, "The Real Mackoys" were descendants of John Mackoy, born in 1722 in King William, Virginia. He was the first Mackoy who changed the spelling of his name from "McCoy." The feuding McCoys lived in the Tug Fork area of Kentucky, while the Real Mackoys lived south of that area in Greenup County, Kentucky. The second record of violence in the feud was in 1878—John Lawson Mackoy moved to Texas in 1876, so "The Real Mackoys" were not party to this infamous conflict.

John Lawson Mackoy was the son of Moses Fuqua Mackoy. Moses Mackoy was born on May 24, 1800 on Kanawha River, West Virginia the third-born son of Lavina Fuqua and John Mackoy. John and Lavina married on January 1, 1795. They later moved to Greenup, County, Kentucky probably around 1801. In Kentucky, John was known as "Deacon" John. The specific area they settled in was called Siloam, and it is situated in a fertile farming section of the Ohio River Valley between the village of Limeville on the east and Mt. Zion on the west. John and Lavina were probably the first settlers in this area and owned 900 acres of land. Deacon John was a founder of the first religious organization in Greenup County. He signed the original records of the Siloam Christian Church that show it being founded in 1819. The congregation met as the "Regular Baptist Church of Tigerts Creek" until 1834, when, evidently through the influence of the teachings of Alexander Campbell, they embraced his doctrine and assumed the name of "The Church of Christ of Tigerts Creek." In January 1840, the minutes of the church state a meeting was held at Siloam Meeting House, which was built on land that was given by John Mackoy. The cemetery can be seen there today. Five generations of Mackoys are buried there. Deacon John's son, Moses Mackoy, is listed as one of the ministers that served this church.[2]

Moses Mackoy was mentioned by my mother a few times because he was known as a preacher and minister who was part of the "Restoration Movement" from which the Churches of Christ originated. I never heard the Mackoy side of my family ever talk about the Mackoys owning slaves in Kentucky, and they did not migrate to Texas until after the Civil War. However, a few years ago I did a search on Newspapers.com, and I found a very interesting story published in 1876 in the Portsmouth Daily Times. It is a story about Moses Mackoy and an incident that began in 1816 or 1817, when Moses would have been 17 years old.

Portsmouth Daily Times—November 18, 1876, by James Keyes

"An incident took place about the year 1816 or 1817 which is worth relating. At the time of which I am speaking, there were a great many negro slaves held by the farmers of Kentucky, and they were very useful in clearing up the heavy timbered lands on the Ohio bottoms. But there were some men in Kentucky, even at that time, who felt a deep sympathy for the downtrodden slave, and thought that something might be done to ameliorate their condition without injury to the interests of slavery. Moses Mackoy was a young man of this description. His father, Deacon John Mackoy, had a large number of slaves of all ages and conditions, and Moses thought there could be no harm in teaching the poor slaves the alphabet and learn them to read the Bible and hymn book, for the negroes are very religious, and excellent singers in their peculiar manner. Accordingly, Moses Mackoy, a young man of seventeen or eighteen years of age, being filled with the spirit of philanthropy towards the down-trodden race of the sons of Africa, gave the negroes of his neighborhood to understand that if

they could procure spelling books and meet him at his father's horse-mill every Sunday morning, he would teach them the mystery of the alphabet and learn them to read and write. They gladly accepted this proposition and met accordingly at the old horse-mill with such books as they could procure, and Moses proceeded to open his school for the instruction of negro slaves in the art of reading and writing, a thing never heard of before in the history of slavery, and contrary to the laws of Kentucky. The school flourished, and Moses was highly gratified to witness the rapid progress that some of his pupils made in the pursuit of their studies. It was but a short time till some of them could read and write very well. It was done so quietly and so little said about it, that the owners of the slaves did not know anything about it, it or took any notice of such a thing as a negro school being carried on in their neighborhood. Mr. King had brought with him from old Virginia a negro boy named Gabriel, who was a very smart, industrious boy and of great use on the plantation. Gabriel attended Moses Mackoy's Sunday School, and soon learned to read and write, and was so fond of practicing is newly acquired art of writing that he could not refrain from writing of the barn door, with a piece of charcoal, such sentences as he had acquired at school.[3]

Portsmouth Daily Times—November 25, 1876, by James Keyes

One day while he was indulged in his propensity for writing, Mr. King caught him at it, and in a very stern manner asked him where he learned that? Gabriel was taken by surprise and not wishing to betray the school hesitated in is reply. Mr. King approached him again in a more threatening manner and demanded to know who it was that learned him to write. Gabriel seeing that matters had come to a crisis and there was no use in trying to evade the question any longer, replied that "Master Moses Mackoy had learned him to read and write! How, when and where did he do it?" "Master Moses had a school up in de ole horse mill every Sunday, and we all goes dar and he teaches us" Mr. King said that it was the most astonishing thing he had ever heard in his life. Why it was against the laws of Kentucky for any white man to learn a negro to read and a heavy penalty was attached to any violation of that act and he would immediately go see Moses and if he was guilty of teaching a negro school he would put a stop to it instanter. So he immediately mounted his horse and rode off post haste to see Moses Mackoy and put a stop to his negro school. Having found Moses who was quietly working on his father's farm and not mistrusting that he had been guilty of any crime, Mr. King, in great excitement, asked him if it was true what Gabriel had said about him. That he had held a negro school and learning all of the young negroes to read and write. Moses acknowledged that there was some truth in the report. That he had held a school every Sunday morning for some time past, and that some of the young negros had learned to read and write a little. Well says Mr. King it is contrary to the laws of Kentucky and if you don't stop it, I will see whether or not the law cannot be enforced against you or not. So Moses had to bring his Sunday School for instruction of the negros to close. But too late, for the poison had been administered and the virus had taken such a hold on the system that not all the laws of Kentucky or any other human power could eradicate it. The negroes had learned to read and they could not be deprived of what they had already attained. This brings to mind an incident which took place in my own school teaching days of long ago before there was any school system or any free schools in the country. I was going from house to house getting subscribers to the school which I was trying to get up according to the old system of subscription schools which is happily no longer in vogue. The country was thinly settled and the people generally very poor. They were very willing to subscribe and glad of an opportunity to give their children a little learning (that dangerous thing that Pope speaks of in his criticism) but how they were to pay for it was the difficulty. One honest old farmer who was *the father of a large family of various ages. Sizes and sexes said to me while putting his name down for several scholars: "There is one thing certain if we will send our children to school and the learning they get can never be taken from then again whether we pay for it or not." I never forgot that observation.*

Mr. King was prosperous as a farmer, accumulated property and became a leading man in the affairs of Greenup County. He was appointed a justice of the peace for the district in which he lived and there was nothing to complain of as to his worldly prospects till about the year 1820. There had been for several years previous a growing disposition among the slaves all along the shores of the Ohio from the head to the mouth of that noble stream to escape from servitude and fly to a country where slavery was not known. They had heard (although their geographical knowledge was quite limited) that such a country existed somewhere within a few days travel which if they could succeed in reaching, they would be forever free of pursuit and would be free forever afterward. To reach this desirable country became the all absorbing wish of every slave held in bondage on the Southern bank of the Ohio. A great many slaves ran away every year. Some were fortunate enough to reach Canada in safety and thus secure their freedom. Others less fortunate were overtaken by their master's and remanded back into servitude. Many an exciting chase took place for recovery of runaway slaves. Sometimes the master would pursue his slave so close that when he would arrive on the shore of the lake he had the satisfaction of bidding his former servant good bye who had got too far from the shore to be brought back. The underground railroad was established about this time for the express purpose of conveying runaway negroes to Canada. Although the railroads above ground had not been heard of at that time it was a great mystery for a long time as to how so many negroes could out-run the fastest horses and make good their escape, but years solved the mystery. It was an underground railroad that did the business.

In the early part of the year 1820, Gabriel took into his head to migrate to a colder climate. The warm and genial atmosphere of Kentucky did not agree with his stout and rugged constitution. He wanted to go where he could do more good at least for himself if not others. So without taking formal leave of any of his friends or even letting them know of the time of his departure he set out for parts unknown. This was a great disappointment to Mr. King who thereby had lost a valuable servant who he had raised from a helpless infant to be valuable to assisting to carry on the heavy work of the plantation. It was very ungrateful on the part of Gabriel to leave his old friends in this unceremonious manner, but selfishness prevailed over gratitude, and he went. Mr. King offered a high reward for his recovery, but nothing was heard from him for several years. On the first of April 1820, the following advertisement appears in the "Scioto Telegraph", a newspaper printed in Portsmouth.

100 DOLLARS REWARD!

Left my house in Greenup County, Kentucky, four miles above Portsmouth, on the 18th of March, 1920, a negro man named

GABRIEL,

About 5 feet 10 inches high, and of a very dark brown or black complexion between 21 and 22 years of age. He has a small scar on his breast occasioned by a burn when young and is very apt to stammer when speaking. His clothing was a London brown broad cloth and linsey pantaloons, swans down waist-coat. Said negro man is supposed by some to be drowned.

Any person finding him alive and delivering him to me shall have the above reward; or fifty dollars for securing him in any jail so that I cannot get him together with all reasonable expenses. If he is drowned anyone finding him will confer a particular favor by writing a few lines to the subscriber directed to Portsmouth post office.

Thomas B. King.

April 1.

Advertising runaway negroes in the newspapers of that day was a very common practice and the publishers generally had a set of cuts on purpose to embellish their advertisements and attract attention, such as a negro with a bundle of clothes in his hand and running at full speed.

Nothing was heard from Gabriel for several years when Moses Mackoy received a letter marked "Canada," when broke the seal he was rejoiced to find it was from Gabriel, one of his former pupils of the old horse mill school which was so abruptly broke up as had been related. Gabriel said that he was in Canada and doing well. He found the negroes there in comfortable circumstances and accumulating property. In consequence of the little schooling, he got in the old horse mill school he had risen to be a leader and schoolteacher among the colored population of that region. He was likewise a preacher of the gospel, but he wished to be a free man with the privilege of going where he pleased, without fear of being remanded back into slavery. He wanted to be a missionary and go among the Southern negroes and preach the gospel to them. He requested Moses Mackoy to have an interview with Mr. King and ascertain what would be the least sum of money he would take and make out his free papers for him. Moses accordingly called on Mr. King and showed him Gabriel's letter and asked him what he would do about it. Mr. King, after revolving the matter in his mind for some time, replied that he supposed Gabriel as lost to him forever, anyhow, and he would name such a sum as he supposed Gabriel would be able and willing to pay for his free papers. He told Moses to write him and tell him if he would send two hundred dollars in cash, he would make out his *papers for him. Moses accordingly wrote to Gabriel as to Mr. King's proposition. It was but a short time till Moses received a letter from Gabriel inclosing two hundred dollars to pay for his emancipation papers. Mr. King made out the papers according to the forms of law in the State of Kentucky. These were duly forwarded and here the matter rested for the present.*

Notwithstanding Gabriel armed with his emancipation papers, was afraid to return to his old home in Kentucky. The dread of slavery could not be shaken off, so he came privately to Portsmouth and secreted himself among some confidential friends of the colored population until he could ascertain how the matter stood on the Kentucky side of the river. He was very anxious to see his old friend Moses Mackoy, but was afraid to venture over for that purpose, but watched his opportunity, expecting to see him in Portsmouth. One day Moses, having some business there was sitting very unconcernedly on a store box, when a tall, young, good looking, well dressed, negro, with the deportment and manners of a gentleman, came up to him and asked him if his name was Moses Mackoy. He replied that it was. Well, said the stranger, I am Gabriel. That was sufficient; the introduction was complete. There was a joyful greeting of old friends about that time, which it is unnecessary to dwell upon here. Every person can imagine the scene to suit himself. They had a long talk together, and Gabriel gave him a full history of his sojourn in Canada and his future movements. He was a regular minister of the gospel and employed by a missionary society to go to the South and preach the gospel to his enslaved brethren, who were held in hopeless bondage and ameliorate their condition as far as lay in his power. To this work he meant to devote himself for the remainder of his life. We will now dismiss Gabriel and say no more about him.

It may be asked by some persons how I came to know all these things? I will state for the benefit of the curious in such matters, that a short time previous to the death of my old friend, Moses Mackoy, it so happened that we were passengers together on a steamboat. We got to talking of incidents which occurred in our schoolboy days and reminiscences of the early times in this country, when he gave me a full history of the Sunday school which he kept in his fathers' old house mill for the benefit of the colored children of his neighborhood, and likewise subsequent career of Gabriel. I had put it in my own language, of course, but the facts are substantially as he related them.[4]

I regret that I never heard this story when I was young person growing up during the 1960s while the civil rights movement was starting America. It would have been beneficial to me to know that my third great grandfather, Moses Mackoy, had taken such a bold step at age 18 to try to significantly improve the plight of Black enslaved people in Kentucky—in 1820! And to realize that he did this as a person who was a Church of Christ minister and who planted churches. This was and is "critical race history." The current movement in states like Texas, Florida, Arkansas, Tennessee, etc., to ban books that deal with our history of race and slavery in America is absurd, repressive, and in my opinion, unchristian. I assume that this autobiography, written by a 7th generation Texan, would be banned from schools in the Lone Star State.

On October 3, 1854, Moses Mackoy met with a small band of Christians to organize a Christian church. Influenced by the teachings of Alexander Campbell, he acted as the shepherd of this flock of believers until April 8, 1855. On that date, the oversight of the congregation was turned over to a group of elders and deacons. Under the direction of these men, the decision was made to move the place of worship to downtown Greenup in March 1857. This congregation still exists and meets at 711 Main Street in Greenup. Moses Mackoy is mentioned in the "About" section on the website of the congregation.

I never heard any of my Mackoy relatives talk about how the family had owned slaves. I had only heard that they had moved to Texas from Kentucky and that they had been farmers. The book *History of Greenup, County, Kentucky* published in 1951 by Nina Mitchell Biggs and Mabel Lee Mackoy says that Deacon John Mackoy had many slaves that he had brought from Virginia. Research done by Ancestry.com revealed that Deacon John Mackoy had fifteen enslaved people in 1830 per the Federal Census:

Age	Males	Females
Under 10 years	1	2
10-23 years	2	4
24-35 years	1	-
36-54 years		3
55-99 years	1	1

The Federal Census of 1840 shows that Deacon John had four enslaved people:

Age	Males	Females
10-23 years	2	1
24-35 years	1	-

This shows that Deacon John has 10 less enslaved people than he did in 1830, so he may have freed, sold, or given away those people. He wrote a will dated June 14, 1842, and the will was "proved" on November 6, 1843, a couple of months after his death. The following statement is in the first paragraph of his will:

> *"I John Mackoy...committing my soul to the Providence of Almighty God with firm belief in Jesus Christ as savior of the world do make this my last will and Testament."*

Then on the next page of the will he "gives" the following enslaved people to his heirs:

- "Black girl named Emaline"
- "Back woman named Juno"
- "Black boy named Isaac"
- "Black boy named Armistead"
- "Black boy named Ben"

Ben was given to Moses Mackoy with the stipulation that Ben could be freed when he could pay $350. Moses was instructed to give the $350 to John's wife Lavina.

It is baffling that Deacon John's belief in "Jesus Christ, as the savior of the world" would allow him to own people and provide him the right "give" them to his heirs as if they were mere possessions.

Now I want to address the history of Moses Fuqua Mackoy's ownership of slaves. The Federal Census of 1830 shows that Moses had five enslaved people:

Age	Males	Females
Under 10 years	2	
10-23 years	2	
24-35 years		1

The Federal Census of 1840 showed Moses had two enslaved people:

Age	Males	Females
10-23 years	1	1

The Federal Census of 1850 showed Moses had two enslaved people:

Age	Males	Females
Under 10 years	1	1

The Federal Census of 1860 showed Moses had five enslaved people:

Age	Males	Females
Under 10 years	1	
10-23 years	3	1

It appears that Moses's sons, John and Henry, did not enslave any people in 1860.

Further research showed that Moses Mackoy sold three enslaved African Americans to G. W. Darlington on March 17, 1834. These were a woman named Milley and her two boys, William and James. One day later, March 18, 1834, Moses and G. W. Darlington agreed that Darlington was to set free Milley and her sons, James and William, starting with Milley on March 17, 1840, and then James on May 15, 1853, and lastly William on October 15, 1859. Moses also freed enslaved Benjamin and Edmund on April 5, 1847. Benjamin was 35 years old and was known as Benjamin Fossett. Edmund was 32 years old and was commonly called Edmund Fossett.

The record of Moses Mackoy owning slaves is very puzzling considering his actions to help slaves with learning literacy when he was 18 years old. Also, it is seems significant that he willingly shared the story of the "underground" literacy school with his friend James Keyes at the end of his life. This quote from the story in the Portsmouth Daily Times comes to mind:

> *"But there were some men in Kentucky, even at that time, who felt a deep sympathy for the downtrodden slave, and thought that something might be done to ameliorate their condition without injury to the interests of slavery. Moses Mackoy was a young man of this disposition."*

The records that have been found show that Moses was involved in the emancipation of several slaves. One could hope the record of him owning younger enslaved people might indicate he was helping them transition out of slavery—but this may be just wishful thinking on my part. I would assume that he was heavily criticized as a young man and was probably, as a result, hesitant to try to publicly advocate change. The laws in Kentucky may have made it difficult to emancipate slaves legally and practically. Moses Mackoy died on August 12, 1869, and the following news item was mentioned in *The Jackson Standard* of Jackson, Ohio:

> *"The Portsmouth papers mention the death of Moses Mackoy of Greenup County Kentucky. He was of the firm of Dugan & Mackoy, Bankers of Portsmouth, and was a father-in-law of Mr. Thomas*

Dugan. He was a preacher of the Christian Order and was a man of excellent character.

My grandfather, Walter Mackoy, was also a family member who helped start and buy the land for a church. He helped found the East Side Church of Christ in Whitesboro, Texas. Whitesboro is a farming town of around 3,000 people and in the late 1950s was a home to three Churches of Christ. This new church was a "split" from the Church of Christ located in downtown Whitesboro. The East Side Church was a splinter movement known as "anti-cooperation" or "non-institutional" churches. The name "non-institutional" refers to Churches of Christ that do not agree with an individual congregation supporting para-church organizations—orphan's homes, colleges, missionaries, etc. In my opinion, this movement in Churches of Christ is tied to the theology of Alexander Campbell and his approach to interpreting the Bible. I will reserve the discussion of his legalist-leaning theology and how it may have significantly influenced the way white Christians justified slavery for a later chapter.

My mother, Pat Mackoy, was a serious, dedicated Christian like her dad. She respected and loved him but disagreed with his position on the "non-institutional" churches. They would have some intense discussions on this topic. Her family might have thought of her as "liberal" when it came to church matters. She was born in 1930 and grew up fairly isolated on a 75-acre farm three miles outside of Whitesboro, Texas. There were not many other children around, and her only contact with the outside world was school. After a few weeks in first grade, she was promoted to second grade because she read so well. Growing up during the Depression, she was poor, but an avid reader interested in learning. She hoped to attend Abilene Christian College upon graduating from Whitesboro High School at age 16. However, her father told her that they could not afford pay for her to attend a private college, so she ended up completing a year of junior college in Texarkana, Texas. A year or so later, an older Mackoy relative who lived in the Dallas area paid for one year at North Texas State University, where she met my dad. She was a serious student of the Bible, and she would read a chapter or two from the Bible to me and my brother every night before bed. While her dad, Walter, might have though she was too liberal in certain church matters, she was strict when it came to the doctrine of Churches of Christ—especially when it came to matters of worship style and what constituted a "true" church. She and I had a few intense discussions on these topics, and I think it was fair to say that she thought I was too liberal in some of my positions. History repeats itself at times.

However, Pat Mackoy was more progressive than her family or church peers when it came to matters of race. When she was 17 years old, she wrote a letter of encouragement to Jackie Robinson, the first African American to play in major league baseball. At that time in the 1950's it was not unusual for me to hear racial slurs used by my white relatives, but such slurs were not tolerated in her house. This a time when women were not granted a lot of say or authority. Without fanfare, she would, on her own, attend Black Churches of Christ Women's conferences that were held in South Dallas. In the 1960s, I heard her have conversations with her parents where she challenged some of their positions on segregation. Unfortunately, she and I did not have any real discussions on this topic while I was growing up at home. She was young—only 20 years older than me—and I do not think she had anyone around her to help her process what was going on with race relations at that time, especially in the context of the culture in Dallas, Texas. As a Bible student, she was involved in teaching classes for women. She and my dad would sometime have Bible studies with couples who were seeking how to become followers of Jesus. She knew the Bible better than most men, but in Churches of Christ, women were to remain silent. On a few occasions she made passing comments that in Churches of Christ the Bible verses talking about the "silence" of women were taken out of context. In 2013, I led a 10-week Bible study regarding the role of women at the Littleton Church of Christ in Colorado that was part of a process of expanding the participation, voice, and leadership of women in that church. It was a controversial topic to study in our church tradition. My mother and father came up one weekend when I was teaching this class on a Sunday night, and I was not sure how my mother would react. She brought a book called "God's Woman" that my grandmother, Winnie Wallis, gave to her when she was young. It talked about how the role of women in the church should be increased. Pat was 82 years old when she attended that Sunday night class. After it was over, she came up to me and said, "I did not think I would live long enough to ever hear this taught in the Church of Christ."

So, where did Pat Mackoy, who grew up on a rural farm in north Texas, ever learn or get the idea that the racial segregation of churches was not right? I don't really know…I wish I had talked to her more about it. I like to think that it was some of that DNA from that 18-year-old Moses Mackoy who in 1820 decided to start an underground literacy school for slaves so that they could read the Bible. I wonder if, when she sat on that farmhouse porch with Sam Mackoy, he said some things that influenced her in that direction.

How did the Mackoys become involved in slavery—the perceived right to own people of another skin color? In March of 2023, I stumbled upon a document on heritage.com. It was a typewritten letter and outline written in 1931 by Mable Mackoy—it led to the source of this horrible institution and practice—the year was 1619.

Chapter 4

1619 POTATO HOLE WOODSONS

Mable Lee Mackoy was born on April 3, 1887, in Kentucky. Moses Mackoy was her 2nd great grandfather, so she is a distant cousin of mine. She never married and lived in Portsmouth, Ohio, for most of her life. She was a co-author of the book *History of Greenup County, Kentucky*, published in 1951.[5] I have a copy of this book that was passed down to me by my mother Patsy Mackoy Wallis. It is very detailed, as it documents the original pioneers and families who came and settled Greenup County, Kentucky.

I have a copy of a letter she wrote on July 25, 1931, to another distant cousin, Harry B. Mackoy, who lived in Cincinnati, Ohio. She mentions that she made a trip in April 1930 to visit relatives in Lynchburg, Virginia. While she was there, she visited the public library, where she discovered an extensive genealogical section. She made a trip to the "quaint little county seat of Campbell County, Rusburg," and she visited with a Mr. Woodson. The letter to Harry Mackoy included four pages of materials that she described as "mostly a conglomeration of notes." Most of the material is from the book *Woodsons and Their Connections* by Henry Morton Woodson.[6] With a quick search on Amazon, I purchased the two-volume set of this book and was able to track her well-organized notes. The following are her comments about the Mackoy family:

"None of the Mackoys live at Siloam, KY, now. The land which they owned for more than 125 years has passed into the hands of strangers. This seems too bad but that part of Kentucky did not progress very fast and as sons and daughters had to go away to get an education they naturally located where there were better opportunities. I think we have reason to be very proud of what the Mackoy's have accomplished. Perhaps we owe more than we realize to John Mackoy and Lavina Fuqua, who must have had a lot of "Grit". Although they probably did not suffer such hardships as the people who came from Virginia to Harrodsburg in the book and movie "The Great Meadow".

Mabel's genealogical investigation of her ancestors beginning in North America are amazing, shocking, and I guess what some people would call "woke." While many in our country today would say I should not be studying the racial history of our family, especially with my grandchildren, how I wish I had known of this history when I was growing up. From five years old, I was taught the Old Testament, with all the good, bad, and the ugly—but not the bad and ugly part of the history of the United States. It was literally "whitewashed."

While in Lynchburg, Mabel Mackoy traced her ancestors back to the time they landed in America for the first time. I will start with our third great grandfather Moses Fuqua Mackoy and list the generations that go back to that event.

Moses Fuqua Mackoy
(My Third-Great-Grandfather)
1800–1869
Third son of John and Lavina Mackoy

Lavina Fuqua Mackoy
1775–1849
Daughter of Judith and Moses Fuqua
Married "Deacon" John Mackoy

Judith Woodson Fuqua

1743–1797

Judith Woodson married Moses Fuqua in 1759.
They went to Kentucky between 1797 and 1800

Obadiah Woodson

1712–1767

Son of Richard Woodson and Ann Smith

Richard F Woodson

1662–1716

Robert Woodson

1634–Unknown

Dr. John Woodson

(MY NINTH GREAT-GRANDFATHER)

1586–1644

Dr. John Woodson was born in 1586 in Dorsetshire, England. He matriculated at St. John's College on March 1, 1604. The family was admitted to bear arms in the reign of Henry VIII. He was part of a large family of students, ministers, teachers, doctors, and lawyers. The maiden name of his wife is unknown, but we know he married her in Devonshire, England. At the age of 33 he came with his wife Sarah and was the surgeon on a ship with Governor Sir George Yeardley to Jamestown, Virginia—in **April of 1619.**

Mabel Mackoy was doing her own 1619 Project in April of 1930.

He located at Fleur de Hundred which is approximately 30 miles north of Jamestown. This area was sometimes called Piersey's Hundred—south side of the James River in Prince George County, Virginia.

Sometime in 1620, a vessel called the *White Lion* landed at Jamestown, carrying about twenty Black captives whom the Dutch skipper had kidnapped somewhere on the coast of Africa.

From the book *Woodsons and Their Connections:*

> *"Referring to Hotten's "Emigrants to America 1600 to 1700" it is seen that our progenitor, John Woodson and his wife, Sara, were registered at Fleur de Hundred, in 1623; and with them were also registered their six African slaves, unnamed and only designated by Roman numerals, thus: I.{ Negor}, II {Negor}, III {Negor}, IV {Negor}, V {Negor}, VI. {Negor}. It is believed that Dr John Woodson bought these six Negroes out of the first importation of African capttives landed at Jamestown, in 1620. From that time until slavery was abolished in the United States, as a result of the Civil War, Dr. John Woodson and his descendants were slave owners."*

Just as America began to be settled, Dr. John Woodson decided to enslave six people from Africa. The right to own other people and submit them to unpaid servitude based on the "myth of white supremacy" took root in American soil and America's "Original Sin" was put into play for generations to come. As the early Americans sought freedom, they took it away from countless others.

The Powhatan Indians led by Opechancanough had conflicted with the English settlers located in Virginia since 1622. On April 18, 1644, Opechancanough led another large-scale attack including Fleur de Hundred where Dr. John Woodson lived. That day, Dr Woodson was returning home from visiting a patient.

Mable Mackoy includes in her notes the basic story of how Dr. John Woodson was killed during that attack on April 18, 1644. The following is a more detailed account of that story written by written by Josephine Rich that is part of an article written by Dallas Bogan in the *LaFollette Press*.[7] I have been unable to find out who Josephine Rich was, but this account is representative of the Woodson family lore that has been passed down through the decades.

The Death of Dr. John Woodson

By Josephine Rich

"As an incentive to colonize America, men received 100 acres of free land when they came to the new world, and that year of 1619, at the first House of Burgess session, Virginia passed a law that wives, too, would receive 100 acres of free land. So Sarah and John chose their 200 acres about 30 miles from Jamestown, across the James River at a place called Fleur de Hundred, now in Prince George County. John and Sarah and their six slaves registered there in 1623.

They had lived first in Jamestown and had come safely through the Jamestown massacre of 1622, and after that John said there would be no further Indian trouble. In fact, they did live without Indian incident for several years at Fleur de Hundred. A son was born to them there in 1632 and another son in 1634.

The Woodson's, like all settlers, owned several guns. The doctor always carried a gun with him on his medical calls and frequently brought home game in his medical saddle bags. The gun that hung over the Woodson log cabin mantelpiece was seven feet six inches long, and had a bore large enough to admit a man's thumb. How anyone could lift it, much less fire it to kill, Sarah had no idea. But she was one day to learn!

The Woodson boys were eight and ten years old on that fateful April 18, 1644. And the boys might have been out in the tobacco fields working that morning, except for the visit of an itinerant shoemaker named Ligon, who was there for his yearly visit to measure the entire household for their year's supply of shoes. Sarah hoped that the doctor would return from his medical call before Ligon the shoemaker had to leave, for the doctor needed a new pair of riding boots.

The spring planting had taken the slaves into the fields so that Sarah and Ligon and the two boys were alone in the cabin when the Indians attacked.

The blood-curdling war whoops rang out and Sarah froze as she looked through the cabin window and saw the feather headdresses come pouring out of the woods. Automatically, Sarah dropped the heavy crossbar on the cabin door. Ligon lifted the seven-foot gun down from the mantelpiece.

An arrow hit a window ledge. Sara bolted the inside shutters on the windows. At the half-story window above in the sleeping loft Ligon poised the giant gun on the window ledge, ready. A powder horn and extra balls lay within hand's reach, ready.

She must hide the boys, Sarah thought, But where? The potato bin hole beneath the cabin floor! It was half empty and tar-kettle dark! It ought to be safe! She lifted the trap door and told one frightened boy to jump, and not to utter a sound.

There was an empty wash tub in the corner of the built-in shed. Eight-year-old Robert might be able to squeeze inside it. He wasn't very big. Sarah told him to squat on the floor. She upturned the wash tub over the boy and then hurried to the hearth to build up the fire under the cooking kettle hanging from fireplace crane. The kettle held the family's supper soup. She added water to fill it to the top and pushed it over the hottest coals. If one of the demon Indians tried to come down the chimney, she had a scalding bath ready.

Looking through a chink in the window shutter Sarah counted nine savages in the howling mob about the cabin. Suddenly her husband appeared, riding out of the forest with his gun ready to fire. Sarah saw him before the Indians did. She let out a cry and then held her breath as she watched.

Before the doctor could shoot, one of the Indians turned and saw him. He aimed and shot his arrow. It struck the doctor, and his gunfire went astray. He fell from his horse and several of the Indians rushed at him waving their battle axes. Sarah covered her eyes.

Ligon's rifle kept cracking. He had gotten three Indians. Sarah watched them fall. Ligon killed five Indians before Sarah heard the noise in the chimney.

They had killed her husband. She was ready to die defending the lives of her sons!

Sarah stood to one side of the hearth with her hand on the kettle. The water scalding, the coals red hot. the Indian came down feet first. Sarah tipped the kettle and gave it to him in full force. He screeched in agony and lay writhing on the floor.

There was more noise up the chimney. Another one was coming down. Sarah grabbed the heavy iron roasting spit. She raised it above her head, holding it with both hands.

As the second Indian stooped to come out of the chimney, Sarah brought her weapon down on his head. It sounded like a pumpkin splitting. He fell heavily to the floor, killed instantly.

She looked up from the bloody bodies to see Ligon unbolting the cabin door.

I'm going to fetch the doctor's body,'" he told her. 'The red devils are finished.'

Sarah counted seven dead Indians in the clearing. The heavy Woodson rifle had served them well.

Although John Woodson had been killed by the Indians, his sons lived to carry on the Woodson name. today, some 300 years later, it is a proud family tradition among the Woodson descendants to be known as either the potato hole Woodsons or the wash tub Woodsons."

For several generations the descendants of the two sons, Robert and Richard, were known as the "The Tub Woodsons" (Robert) and the "The Potato Hole" Woodsons (Richard).

The following is a description of the Woodson family included in Mabel Mackoy's notes. She sourced this from Henry Morton Woodson's book, *Woodsons and Their Connections.*

> *"The family is a widespread one of good people. Godfearing and loving, frugal and industrious and "given to hospitality". Many of the men have held high postitions, and no race or tribe has ever produced women more beautiful, more self-sacrificing, more unbending in their fidelity to duty and the dictates of conscience. Our capable women have never been distinguished for a sweet dignity that is altogether without austerity."*

Henry Morton Woodson also makes this statement regarding the fact that, from the time Dr. John Woodson enslaved six Africans in 1620 until the end of the Civil War, he and his descendants were slave owners:

> *"So far as I have been able to learn, they were humane masters, recognizing their slaves as personal property, caring for them as valuable property and treating them as human beings."*

The above statement, made in 1915, is based in the full-blown belief in the myth of white supremacy. It is such an arrogant statement that reeks of a complete lack of self-awareness. In the second edition of his 2018 book, *Myths America Lives By: White Supremacy and the Stories That Give Us Meaning,* Richard T. Hughes outlines the following "great American myths" that have hardened and absolutized into rigid orthodoxies from which we often permit little or no dissent:[8]

- The Myth of a Chosen Nation—the notion that God Almighty chose the United States for a special mission for the world

- The Myth of Nature's Nation—the conviction that American ideals and institutions are rooted in the natural order, that is, in God's own intentions first revealed at the dawn of creation

- The Myth of the Millennial Nation—the notion that the United States, building on that natural order, will usher in a final golden age for all humankind

- The Myth of a Christian Nation—the claim that America is a Christian nation, consistently guided by Christian values

- The Myth of the Innocent Nation—the conviction that, while other nations may have blood on their hands, the nobility of the American cause always redeems the nation and renders it innocent

Hughes summarizes the argument in his book this way:

> *"First the Myth of White Supremacy is the primal American myth that informs all the others and, second, that one of the chief functions of the other five myths is to protect and obscure the Myth of White Supremacy, to hide it from our awareness, and to assure us that we remain innocent after all."*

The story of Dr. Woodson also involves the occupation of a foreign land by the British and the ultimate dislocation and killing of the majority of Indigenous people that were already living in America. This "original sin" is also based in the "myth of white supremacy."

It appears that karma was not on Dr. Woodson's side the afternoon of April 16, 1644.

Richard Woodson survived the attack that day in 1644, and the practice of slavery survived with his descendants for another 221 years.

The current 1619 Project led by Nicole Hannah-Jones is an important message of properly looking at a new origin story of the United States of America. Hannah-Jones says this in the introduction to *The 1619 Project: A New Origin Story*:

"Why hadn't any teacher or textbook, in telling the story of Jamestown, taught us the story of 1619? No history can ever be complete, of course. Millions of moments, thousands of dates weave the tapestry of a country's past. But I knew immediately, viscerally, that this was not an innocuous omission. The year white Virginians first purchased enslaved Africans, the start of American Slavery, an institution so influential and corrosive that it both helped create the nation and nearly led to its demise, is indisputably a foundational historical dated. And yet I'd never heard of it before."[9]

Why had my family not told the story of Mabel Lee Mackoy's genealogical research that she did in Virginia back in 1930? The story reveals the history of slavery in our family going back to 1620. Instead, we were immersed in a "myth of innocence," ironically wrapped with generational belief in fundamental Christianity.

I am a descendant of the "Potato Hole Woodsons."

Chapter 5

THE GREAT MEADOW

M abel Mackoy writes in her letter of July 25, 1931, to her cousin Harry that "John Mackoy and Lavina Fuqua had a lot of "Grit." She was referring to the couples' move from Campbell County Virginia to Kentucky around 1800. Mabel references the book and movie *The Great Meadow*, about the story of a young couple who set out on Daniel Boone's wilderness route across the Appalachian highlands to Kentucky. The Indigenous people referred to the area of Kentucky as "The Great Meadow." After the Revolutionary war most of the desirable land in Virginia was taken and many people were ready to try a new land. They had heard reports of fur traders and adventurers like Daniel Boone about the many rivers, grassy plains, and abundant forests of "The Great Meadow." A lot of the early pioneers following the Ohio River came to a big bend that was a broad valley enclosed by green hills. They decided that this northeastern section of Kentucky would be a favorable place to live. In addition, this area was not occupied by Indigenous people. These English and Scotch-Irish farmers whose ancestors had come to Virginia decided to settle this "new land." Plenty of timber was found in the hills that was suitable for building houses, barns, and mills. In addition, in those hills they found coal for fuel, stones for various construction projects, and iron and other minerals.[10]

Lavina Fuqua Mackoy was the daughter of Captain Moses F. Fuqua, a descendant of the French Huguenots of Virginia and was also a Revolutionary soldier. Mabel Mackoy's writings provide a brief history of the Fuqua Family and states that the records she found were accepted by the "Huguenot Society of Pa." The Fuquas were Huguenot refugees from France. In France, the Christians who espoused the doctrines of the Reformation that began in Europe with Martin Luther and John Calvin were called Huguenots. The ruling powers of France persecuted the Huguenots for more than a hundred years. Beginning in the late 1600s they began fleeing to America. The following is a story told by two granddaughters of Moses Fuqua, Jr., as recorded by Mabel Lee Mackoy:

> *"The Fuqua family in France consisted of father, mother and baby son, and a nurse maid. They were planning to escape the persecution of the Catholics, by joining a party of persons who were leaving on a boat for America. They were to slip out of their house through a basement door after dark, taking only the clothes and what money they possessed. The money was concealed on the person of the nurse. All were in the basement except the father who was still in the house. They heard a noise, and the mother went upstairs to see what had happened and found that the Catholics had come and killed their father. They also killed her. The nurse escaped with the baby and went to the boat as they had planned. There she found friends among the passengers by the name of McClure, Dr. McClure's family. He took charge of the baby, and the money, using it to pay for the child's needs until he was a grown man. The young Fuqua married Dr. McClure's daughter. He took care of the old nurse until her death. This is supposed to be the first Fuqua in America. They landed in Virginia."...Mabel Lee Mackoy*

Captain Moses Fuqua (who married Judith Woodson) bought more than 1,000 acres of land in Greenup County, Kentucky, above the mouth of Tygart Creek in 1799. Captain Fuqua was old man at that time, so he sent his son Moses Fuqua, Jr., to see the land and set up a place for the family to live. *The History of Greenup County Kentucky* describes the move from Virginia:

"Moses Fuqua Jr. returned to Virginia, made his report of the land to his father, and in due time the large family with their many slaves came to Kentucky. Moses Fuqua Sr.'s wife, Judith Woodson, died just before they left for Virginia."

"Deacon" John Mackoy came to Kentucky with his wife Lavina, daughter of Moses Fuqua, Sr. They moved from Virginia to Greenup County, Kentucky, around 1800 and made their home in the Siloam neighborhood near the Fuqua family farm.

The pioneers who came from Virginia to Greenup County brought their enslaved people with them. The 1931 movie *The Great Meadow,* however, depicts no enslaved Black people included in the group making the difficult trek across the Appalachian Mountains to Kentucky. [11] Nevertheless, thousands of enslaved people in chains came to Kentucky through the Cumberland Gap along that rugged Wilderness Trail. The men were handcuffed and chained together in long lines and led women and children who walked behind. These enslaved people were key in building the new homes, church buildings, mills, and working the farmlands in Greenup County Kentucky.

The Mackoy and Fuqua families were listed as members of the Siloam Christian Church that began in 1819 and that became the Church of Christ of Tigerts Creek in 1834. They brought their Christian orthodoxy, and they brought their slaves to The Great Meadow.

The following quote is part of the description of "Slavery in Greenup County" found in the book, *The History of Greenup County, Kentucky.*

"The Negroes were well mannered, and they were well treated by their masters. There were none of the evils of slavery that existed in some sections of Kentucky, no slave auction block nor whipping post. It is true they were bought and sold, as elsewhere in the South, but it was done in a decent and orderly manner."

This statement is typical of the way the peculiar institution of slavery was described in Kentucky. It was like saying, we do have slavery—but at least we're not Mississippi or Alabama. White people in Kentucky promoted the

"Happy Slave Myth" and have glossed over what really happened in that state. To be clear, the selling of children, husbands, wives, and friends was in no way orderly or decent—it was evil.

> *"Slavery in Kentucky was not a mild form of servitude, for, to the modern mind no such condition existed. Slavery was a heinous evil for everyone it touched, regardless of the degree of degradation. But there are, of course, graduations within systems, even the "peculiar institution." It does not excuse those systems to explain such differences. To state that slaves fared better in Kentucky's slave system as compared to that of the Deep South does not exonerate the evil of both systems. Under slavery, generalizations are exceptionally hard to make and easily misunderstood, for exceptions are numerous. Yet to understand slavery, in all its cruel aspects, requires both general generalizations and attempts at analysis of graduations. One generalization is easy: slavery was a system where one race controlled another, where psychological as well as physical restraints and wounds abounded. For, once a slave, you would always be a slave, subject to others. Of that fact, statements of degree of harshness pale into insignificance. For even if well treated, as many Kentuckians, black and white, claimed slaves knew that freedom was a distant dream—and, for most only a dream. Of that they were sure."*

> —Marion B. Lucas.[12]

The Mackoy, Floyd, and Fuqua families brought their enslaved people to Kentucky from the state of Virginia—where the peculiar institution of slavery began. In 1662, Virginia enacted a law that said that black women's children would be held free, or bond based exclusively on the condition of the mother—meaning all children of a Black slave would be slaves for life. In 1667, Virginia enacted a law that declared that the baptism of an enslaved person did not exempt them from bondage. The Virginia code of 1705 declared the following:

- "All Negro, mulatto and Indian Slaves within this dominion shall be held to be real estate. If any slave resists his master and the master shall happen to kill such slave in correction of that slave...the master shall be free of all punishment as if such accident never happened"

- Inter-racial marriage was declared illegal
- Slaves needed written permission to leave plantations
- Slaves could receive harsh physical punishments since enslaved people had no ability to pay fines

In 1773, the Virginia colony enacted a law that denied free Blacks the right to vote or carry any sort of weapons. Virginia then passed a law in 1750 defining the distinction between slave and servant, regulating all slaves to the status of property.

The new freedoms of "The Great Meadow" found by the white pioneers did not belong to enslaved black people. White Kentuckians wrote their first state constitution in 1792. While abolitionists existed and protested at that time, the majority incorporated their white supremacist views into the new constitution, stating that all the laws of Virginia regarding slavery were in force in Kentucky. This meant that the enslaved Blacks that came from Virginia and all female bondswomen were slaves in Kentucky. In 1798, the Kentucky legislature adopted a comprehensive slave code with regulated all Blacks, both freepersons and slaves, to an inferior position to every part of life in the State of Kentucky. All of this was based on the view that white people were superior to Black people and that Black people were born permanently into slavery.

There were Kentuckians who opposed slavery from the early days of Kentucky statehood, but they were not able to accomplish any significant changes. Slavery's future received attention and debate at the 1849 Kentucky constitutional convention but nothing significant was accomplished to modify or end the institution of slavery. The following statement was included in the final document of the 1849 convention:

"The right of property is before and higher than any constitutional sanction, and he right of an owner of a slave to his property is

the same and inviolate as the right of an owner of any property whatsoever"[13]

The enslavement of Black people was not something that just "naturally" happened. It was debated "on the record" in the constitutional conventions, state legislatures, federal legislators, among theologians and in newspapers of the day. It did not just evolve with both whites and Blacks agreeing that this was the way God intended it. It was ruthlessly pursued and prosecuted by white people to the point of a supposed "Christian Nation" entering a Civil War to keep the "peculiar institution." In Kentucky, Black people were considered chattel property and not human beings.

Kentucky's economy was one of small self-sufficient farms in contrast to the South, where 25% of the enslaved population lived on plantations where each had at least 100 slaves. The average master of the 38,000+/- masters in Kentucky, had about five slaves. The enslaved worked as farmers, handymen, cattlemen and merchants. Enslaved people plowed the fields, raised corn, sweet potatoes, and wheat along with the cash crops of tobacco, kemp, and flax. Their labor was the driving force that made Kentucky a prosperous antebellum state.

The field hands had very tough and demanding jobs where they had the most monotonous and boring experiences. There workday began at dawn and ended at dusk with an hour or two of rest during the heat of the day. Females were often made to work in the fields especially during harvest time. Working the hemp fields was the hardest and dirtiest task for field hands. Hemp was tied to the booming cotton industry in the South because the hemp was used to make rope for use in tying up cotton bales.

In addition, enslaved Blacks built roads, canals, bridges—wherever their labor was needed. They also worked as waiters, cooks, and maids. Children were also expected to work, and they transitioned to full work by around 14 to 15 years of age. The children of a female slave were the property of her owner regardless of the status of their father.

Slave cabins were typically built of logs and had brick or stone fireplaces. They often only had one door, sometimes with no windows and the cabin floors were almost always dirt. A family would typically live in a cabin that was a single room from around 100 to 275 square feet with a dirt floor. The windows were often crude "holes" that had to be covered with bark shutters to prevent rain from blowing into the room. Typically for those who lived on small farms, the females cooked meals in the cabin fireplace or in the yard when weather permitted.

The slaves wore homespun clothes that were typically made of course flax fibers and were generally handed out annually with little variation between summer and winter. House servants might receive hand-me-downs. The men would wear trousers and shirts and the women cheap calico skirts and houses. Clothing was often handed out annually and shoes often wore out before a year was out.

Kentucky law strictly regulated the mobility of slaves and required slaves who were away from their residences for longer than four hours to have a pass—which effectively restricted enslaved people to a distance between eight to ten miles from their home. The passes could only be issued by members of the slave owner's family or by employers or overseers. State law fixed a slave's punishment for not having a pass at "ten lashes on his or her bare back." Slaves who contemplated clandestine "unlawful assemblies" faced arrest by any white citizen who discovered them and severe punishment by the state. The enslaved people were typically required to work half a day on Saturday, but they were given Sundays off and they could spend that time socializing or attending church services.

Most enslaved people of Kentucky discerned that to receive good treatment they had to do what their masters told them to do. So, they would develop a working relationship with their master that would allow them to survive. A enslaved man named George Dunn told of receiving reasonably good treatment by his owners...he remembered being "whipped only once." Another enslaved man named David Barrett said in a 1837 interview that he "could not complain of harsh treatment" from his master. Lewis Bibb, an enslaved man who was interviewed in Louisville in 1863, described his owner as a "rightly good man." However, Dunn, Barrett, and Bibb all eventually fled from their owners as fugitives.

In Kentucky, the most common form of punishment given by owners to enslaved persons was whipping. Almost all slaveholders kept whips to enforce their authority and most used them. The whips that were used for adults were a strip of twisted, tapered, rigid cow hide. A hickory switch was used on the legs of children. This was a time when corporal punishment was the norm. "Bucking" was a method used when whipping slaves. The slaves' hands were tied together in front and then forced over the persons legs while sitting down. A three-and-a-half-foot stick was then slid under the persons knees, but above his arms—locking the enslaved person in a position that exposed his back. Both men and women were whipped.

The enslaved people of Kentucky did not benefit from the traditional Christian "family values" that were taught in the churches. Under both the Virginia and Kentucky state constitutions slave marriages were unrecognized by the law. The children of female slaves were the property of her owner regardless of the status of their father. Parental relationships with children were wholly dependent upon the whims of the owner. They could be sold at any time. The enslaved Black people of Kentucky fell in love and wanted to be married—like all people do—but the permission to marry had to be granted by the enslaved couples' owners. Many times, the man and women had different owners which complicated the arrangement. The couples who lived on separate farms would only be allowed to see each other on the weekends. The worst and most abhorrent aspect of slavery was the destruction of families when men, women and children were sold separately—especially if they were sold to the Deep South. The term "sold down the river" has been used for generations to describe a profound betrayal. Louisville, Kentucky, was one of the largest slave-trading places in the country and that activity brought significant wealth to that city. The importation of African American slaves was ended in the United States by 1808, but a global demand for cotton clothing caused a huge demand for labor in the Deep South of the United States. This resulted in over one million enslaved people who were born in the "slave-growing states" (such as Kentucky) to be sold to the Deep South between 1790 and 1860. "The River" was a literal reference to the Ohio and Mississippi rivers. The planters preferred men over women as laborers so the sale of men to the South would cause the tragedy of separating and breaking up of families. White families who had mounting debts would often sell some of their slaves to pay off their debts. A famous black preacher, Rev. London Ferrill, would include in the enslaved marriage nuptials the phrase: *"married until death or parted by distance."*[14]

In Kentucky, slaveowners would often "hire out" their slaves when they had a surplus of slaves and would often hire out the enslaved children. This "hiring out" also disrupted the family unit. In addition, the people who "rented" the slaves often provided a harsher and lower standard of care to those slaves. These "renters" did not own them and were not "at risk" for their long-well-being. This practice of "hiring out" also split up enslaved families for significant amounts of time.

In the Great Meadow Blacks experienced significantly substandard living conditions and were not paid for their labor. White people in Kentucky believed in the inferiority of Blacks and would not even recognize the legal right for them to marry. Without mercy, they were willing to break up families and "sell them down the river." It boiled down to the love of money rather than loving their neighbor.

The Fuqua family line narrowly escaped the persecution of the Catholics to American soil where they were able to have hope for a new life. However, the Black people who they then enslaved on American soil did not have that hope. Kentucky enslaved people had nothing to look forward to other than the end of the workday and to the fear of losing family members. But remarkably, the Black people of Kentucky built their own society and love of family and church. They did not just have grit. They had true grit.

Each year, on the first Saturday in May, Kentucky runs the internationally famous thoroughbred horse race known as the Kentucky Derby. Each year before the trumpets call the horses and riders to the starting gate, the large crowd gathered there sings the iconic, nostalgia-laden song, "My Old Kentucky Home." Here are the original lyrics of that song:

MY OLD KENTUCKY HOME, GOOD NIGHT!

Stephen Foster, 1853

The sun shines bright in the old Kentucky home,

'Tis summer, the darkies are gay,

The corn-top's ripe and the meadow's in the bloom,

While the birds make music all the day.

The young folks roll on the little cabin floor,

All merry, all happy and bright;

By'n by Hard Times comes a knocking at the door,

Then my old Kentucky Home, good night!

Chorus

Weep no more my lady,

Oh! Weep no more today!

We will sing one song

For the old Kentucky Home,

For the old Kentucky Home, far away.

They hunt no more for the possum and the coon,

On a meadow, the hill and the shore,

They sing no more by the glimmer of the moon,

On the bench by the old cabin door.

The day goes by like a shadow o'er the heart,

With sorrow, where all was delight:

The time has come when the darkies have to part,

Then my old Kentucky home, good night!

Chorus

The head must bow and the back will have to bend,

Wherever the darky may go:

A few more days, and the trouble will all end,

In the fields where the sugar-canes grow,

A few more days for to tote the weary load,

No matter 'twill never be light;
A few more days till we totter on the road,
Then my old Kentucky home, good night!
Chorus

This song that is loved by many white people is about slavery and Black people being "sold down the river" to the Deep South. In her book *My Old Kentucky Home—The Astonishing Life and Reckoning of an Iconic American Song* Emily Bingham says this:

> *"My Old Kentucky Home" is a spy hole into one of America's deftest and most destructive creations: the "singing slave" whose song assured hearers that the plantation was happy and a place where Black people belonged. Its beginning lines establish a toxic illusion of contented bondage. Later verses take as settled fact that "the head must bow and the back will have to bend, Wherever the darky may go." Its comforting chorus enacts the lie that people forced into slavery were unresisting, unmanned, perversely grateful.*[15]

The story of my family history has been primarily framed around my American ancestors being founding members of the Church of Christ and that they were solid Americans—good pioneer stock. But the story of family history told regarding slavery was minimal and almost nonexistent at times. The story that was an illusion of a "happy" time for black enslaved people who were supposedly content.

The following is a list of my family ancestors who lived in Kentucky:

(In addition, I have noted those who also lived in Virginia or Texas)

Kentucky Ancestors:

5th Great

- Moses F. Fuqua (Virginia)

4th Great

- Deacon John Mackoy (Virginia)

- Lavina Fuqua Mackoy (Virginia)
- David Saunders (Virginia)
- Elizabeth Page Saunders (Virginia)
- John M. Lawson (Virginia)
- Susannah Blue Lawson (Virginia)
- David Floyd (Virginia)
- Catherine Burdett Floyd (Virginia)

3rd Great

- John B. Floyd (Texas) (
- Julia Ann Lindsay Floyd Texas)
- Joseph Broad (Texas)
- Artamesa Cooper Broad (Texas)
- John Huffines, Sr .(Texas)
- Elizabeth Wright Huffines (Texas)
- Thomas Drewery Saunders (Virginia)
- Mildred Mimms Saunders (Virginia)
- Moses Fuqua Mackoy, Sr. (Virginia)
- Hannah Lawson Mackoy (Virginia)

2nd Great

- James Lindsay Floyd (Texas)
- Alice Artimesia Broad Floyd(Texas)
- John Thomas Saunders (Texas)
- Francis Huffines Saunders (Texas)
- John Lawson Mackoy (Texas)
- Mary Eliza Mackoy (Texas)

Great

- Samuel Walter Mackoy (Texas)

A total of 26 of my relatives on the above list lived in Kentucky. That is a significant "host of witnesses." However, I never heard my family talk much at all about our Kentucky roots. The narrative was limited to "the Mackoys were from Kentucky and there was a cemetery located in Greenup County, Kentucky, where several generations of Mackoys were buried." The emphasis was that we were from the "Great State of Texas," and that was what really mattered. But "The Great Meadow" was very influential in the culture that was built by these settlers in North Texas. Jim Schutz said this about the early settlers of Dallas in his 1986 book *The Accommodation—The Politics of Race in an American City*:

> *"For the most part and most of the time, the core people and culture that settled Texas was ferociously resolute and sober, the ultimate distillate and essence of the Emersonian dream—a sturdy race of ascetically religious American small farmers marching into the wilderness with guns and Bibles in their hands, a truly courageous and indomitable people, bent on holding land and making good, and daunted by not one dammed thing. They also happened to be from a fairly narrow ethnic pool that didn't get much broader the longer they stayed out on the frontier."*[16]

My family roots are from "a fairly narrow ethnic pool" that is steeped with the Southern culture of Kentucky and Virginia. In addition, my family heritage is a "fairly narrow religious pool" of families that were members of the Restoration Churches that had their origins in Kentucky. These people lived close together in Kentucky and then even closer in North Texas. I think it is reasonable to say that there was not a lot of diversity of thought, and this encouraged a naive confidence in believing they were uniquely "right" in their religious thinking and that there was no practical need to question the history of slavery...or the greatness of Texas.

Currently, at the Kentucky Derby, they only sing the first verse of "My Old Kentucky Home" to do away with the song's slavery roots—so that we can be "okay" with it. Emily Bingham ends her book with the following statement:

"My Old Kentucky Home" has been handed down and held up as a thing to cherish, a hallowed ritual, a delight to me and countless others who have infused it with emotional warmth. But that legacy is not reason to ask, why would anyone question it."

I never have thought of Kentucky as "my old home," and I have never thought much about that song. But realizing the inevitable influence of my family roots from the culture of Kentucky has caused me to think more critically about the message delivered by that song. It provides insight into how the Floyds would come to use the phrase "Happy Slaves." The well documented and even "revered" legacy of my Kentucky ancestors being founders of Christian churches should not provide me with a reason to not ask critical questions regarding their involvement with the institution of slavery. It is a profound contradiction.

I assume that "My Old Kentucky Home" will still be played at the Kentucky Derby and other traditional events in that state. I hope that it will be heard as a song of "lament"—not as a celebration of an over-warmed nostalgia of a mythic "happy" time that really did not exist in Kentucky. On the contrary the "Great Meadow provided a hard life for Black enslaved people. Like the French Huguenots who came to Kentucky—those who were enslaved also wanted to be free to pursue their own dreams.

Chapter 6

NEW YEAR'S EVE, 1831

My family heritage is deeply rooted in the Church of Christ, a religious movement rooted in what is commonly referred to as the Stone-Campbell movement. The movement is named after two ministers and church planters, Barton W. Stone (1772–1844) and Alexander Campbell (1788–1866). The formation of these two movements happened primarily between 1801 and 1831. The following religious groups today have their origins in the Stone-Campbell movement:

- Disciples of Christ/Christian Church
- Independent Christian Churches
- Churches of Christ

These two movements could be considered the first nondenominational churches in America. They had no formal hierarchy and autonomous congregations were locally led by a plurality of men called elders along with a minister/preacher. The first group started by Barton W. Stone began in 1801 at the Cane Ridge Meeting in Paris, Kentucky. They were called Christians only to restore the original name used in the New Testament for followers of Jesus of Nazareth. The second group led by Thomas Campbell and his son Alexander began in what is now West Virginia and they called themselves Disciples of Christ.

Both groups generally held these beliefs in common:

- Jesus is the Christ, the Son of God.

- Baptism of adult believers by immersion in water is required to become a Christian.

- Christians should gather each Sunday to partake of Communion.

- They hold the Bible in high regard— "we speak where the Bible speaks and are silent where the Bible is silent."

- Without church hierarchy, they are made up of autonomous local congregations.

In 1831 in Georgetown, Kentucky, a few leaders from churches of each of the two groups began meeting to discuss the merger of congregations from the two movements. They decided to have set of meetings to seriously discuss the possibility of a merger to begin on Friday, December 30, 1831. They anticipated a large crowd, so they set the meeting at the Hill Street Church in Lexington, Kentucky. The next day, December 31, 1831, "Racoon" John Smith spoke on behalf of the "Campbell churches" and Barton W. Stone spoke on behalf of the congregations he started. The meeting ended with the two shaking hands and the movements joined as one. The congregations would be known as "Christian Churches" or "Churches of Christ."[17]

I am a seventh-generation member of the Church of Christ. While there is no recorded list of attendees, it is possible some of my forefathers were there on New Year's Eve 1831. Here are four possible relatives who might have been in attendance:

From Trimble County, Kentucky—80 miles from Lexington

- John B. Floyd:18 yrs. old, 3rd great-grandfather

- Joseph Broad:18 yrs. old, 3rd great-grandfather

From Greenup County, Kentucky—120 miles from Lexington

- "Deacon John" Mackoy: 59 yrs. old, 4th great-grandfather

- Moses Mackoy-31 yrs. old, 3rd great-grandfather

(Note: The reason no females are listed is because they were most likely not invited—they were to be silent in church meetings.)

Moses Mackoy was a well-known Church of Christ minister and student of Alexander Campbell. John B. Floyd and Joseph Broad became founding trustees of the Richardson Church of Christ in 1874. Out of the four, I think it is most likely Moses Mackoy that was in attendance because of his age and his role as a minister in the Campbell church movement. It's also likely that his father, "Deacon" John Mackoy, would have gone with Moses to the meeting. Even if they were not present, they would certainly have been aware of its importance. They became part of the Church of Christ. So, my roots in the Church of Christ go all the way back to the unity meeting in Lexington, Kentucky, on New Year's Eve, 1831. At that time the membership of those churches was about 20,000, and that grew to nearly 200,000 in 1860.

As this group grew, it was known as the "Restoration Movement." The goal was to restore the church back to its original form as it was in the first century. It was not unusual to see a Church of Christ building built in the 1950s with a cornerstone bearing the following engraving: "Established Pentecost, A.D. 33." When I was growing up in the Church of Christ I never heard much about the Stone-Campbell movement, but instead would hear we were a "First Century" church, and we followed the ancient Scriptures of the Bible as our sole guide. It seemed like there was no need to discuss the Restoration Movement's origins in America. In our minds, we had leaped back 2,000 years to the original church and avoided the perceived "apostacy" of the Catholics, Lutherans, Anglicans, etc. In this chapter, I want to specifically discuss the movement's attitudes towards slavery in the United States. I will focus mainly on the teachings of Barton W. Stone and Alexander Campbell regarding slavery in the context of living a Christian life.

Barton W. Stone was probably the most outspoken Church of Christ leader to explicitly state his opposition to the institution of slavery existing in America. In his autobiography, Stone tells of trip he made when he was 25 years old from Kentucky to Virginia and eventually Charleston. He tells of this encounter with slavery:

> *"Before I reached Charleston, I passed over Stone River into John's and Wadmelaw islands. There I remained some days and received the most friendly attention of gentlemen professing religion, living in splendid places, surrounded with a rich profusion of luxuries, and of everything desirable; the pleasures were heightened by free, humble and pious conversation. But in the midst of all the glory, my soul sickened at the sight of slavery in more horrid forms than I had ever seen before; poor negroes! Some chained to their work—some wearing iron collars—all half naked and followed and driven by the merciless lash of a gentleman overseer—distress appeared scowling in ever face. This was the exciting cause of my abandonment of slavery."* [18]

In 1834, Stone moved his family from Kentucky to Jackson, Illinois. One of the reasons for moving to this northern state was so his wife could free the slaves she inherited from her mother. After suffering through an extended illness, Stone spoke in his autobiography about the decision that their slaves should be freed:

> *"I immediately put on dry clothes, went to bed, slept comfortably, and rose the next morning relieved from the disease which had baffled medicine, and threatened my life. That night's sweat was my cure, by the grace of God. I was soon able to renew my ministerial labors and was joyful to see religion progressing. This happy state of things continued for some time and seemed to gather strength with days. My mind became unearthly and was solely engaged in the work of the Lord. I had emancipated my slaves from a sense of right, choosing poverty with a good conscience, in preference to all the treasures of the world. This revival cut the bonds of many poor slaves; and this agreement speaks volumes in favor of the work. For of what avail is a religion of decency and order, without righteousness?"* [19]

Stone's reasons for opposing slavery were not sourced from a legalistic reading of the Bible, considering it a matter of "mere opinion" or the belief in the "supremacy of the white race." Instead, it came from the following teaching of Jesus:

> *"Love the Lord your God with all your heart and with all your soul and with all your mind and with all your strength.'[[31] The second is this: 'Love your neighbor as yourself.' There is no commandment greater than these."*

> —*Mark 12: 30-31, NIV*

He felt physically ill when he observed the terrible treatment of the slaves near Charleston. He felt empathy for these people. He also recognized a significant reason white Americans were not willing to do away with the enslavement of Black people: "financial wealth," when he said he chose "poverty over the financial riches that slavery provided to him."

In 1800, prior to the merger of the Stone and Campbell groups, Barton Stone wrote an antislavery resolution for the West Lexington Presbytery. It called out slavery as a moral evil and said members of the church who practiced slavery should not be part of the church. In 1835, Stone began working with the publication of a tract by the New England Anti-Slavery Convention. In that tract, Stone says slavery is the darkest cloud hanging over America and if not removed it would burst into ruinous desolation. However, he stopped publishing the tract because of the protest of friends and patrons in the South. Stone could not see a clear solution to the problem of slavery and was not willing to risk the possible conflict that could lead to division in the churches.

Stone eventually did pursue a solution to the problem of slavery in the United States. While living in Kentucky he witnessed firsthand the poor living conditions of Black people and even worse was that Black people had no freedom and could not advance financially or socially in the United States. Around 1839, he supported the idea of establishing a colony in Liberia where slaves could go to establish a new life—if their slaveholders would grant them their freedom. He worked with the American Colonization Society, but it had division within and was attacked by abolitionists from the outside. Stone eventually became disappointed in the Society and was no longer significantly involved. This "solution" did not consider that most Black people considered themselves American pioneers and they wanted to be set free in the country they had helped build.

Stone personally did act proactively against slavery by freeing his wife's slaves and calling out slavery as evil. However, in the 1830s the Restoration churches were more interested in maintaining church unity than ending slavery. The lack of any sort of formal church hierarchy prevented the platforms to properly wrestle with the evils of slavery. Barton Stone died in 1844 and did not witness the horrors of the Civil War 17 years later.

Alexander Campbell was probably the most prominent and well-known leader of the Restoration Movement. He was born in Ireland in 1788 and was of Scottish descent. He was educated at the University of Glasgow and then emigrated to the United States where he joined his father who had emigrated in 1807 and was a minister. He lived in Bethany, Virginia, on a significant farm his wife inherited from her father. After the birth of his first daughter, he came to believe the Bible did not support infant baptism. He taught that baptism of adult believers by immersion in water is required to become a Christian. Campbell was an avid writer, and he was a publisher of two widely distributed journals:

- 1823–1830—*The Christian Baptist*
- 1830–1866—*The Millennial Harbinger*

My third-great grandfather, Moses Mackoy, is mentioned twice in *The Millennial Harbinger*:

- *March 1855—"Bro. S. S. Doyle, evangelist for the Greenup and Portsmouth Co-operation, reports, February 2nd, 35 additions, all by immersion, during a protracted meeting of ten days, at Greenupsburg, Ky. Bros. Moses M'Koy and the Doyle were the speakers"*

- *February 1857—Moses McKoy, at a meeting on the second Lord's Day in October 1856, at Union Meeting House, in Greenup County Kentucky, had twenty additions, and organized a congregation of thirty-two members.*

Campbell also wrote several books and participated in debates, some of which gained national attention.

Alexander Campbell was an academic and one who generally read the Bible with a "literal view." His position on slavery over the years was at best mixed, and he viewed it from a legalistic and analytical mindset. Unlike Stone, Campbell displayed no empathy for the plight of Black people in America. In 1832, Campbell said in the *Christian Baptist* that the system of slavery was the most inconsistent of all the paradoxes of Christianity and was one of the blackest spots on the nation and left it at that. In the 1830s the leaders in the Restoration believed there were more important religious issues than slavery and took what some called the "middle ground." They would not condemn the slaveholder as wrong just because he owned slaves, but they generally still refused to bless the institution of slavery. It was considered a political question that the government, not the church, should deal with.

In 1845, Campbell published a series of articles regarding slavery in hope that the members of the Church of Christ would align with his positions. He stated that slavery was permitted by the Bible, but the treatment of the slaves by white slaveholders had to be in accordance with the teaching of the Bible. He did admit that most white slaveholders were not able to practice slavery in accordance with Christian principles. He also criticized the abolitionists as being too extreme and that neither a Christian...or an American citizen... could be an abolitionist. His convoluted position was that he was antislavery, but he would not be an abolitionist who was willing to sacrifice everything to pursue that goal. In 1850, Campbell supported the harsh Fugitive Slave Laws as constitutional and said they agreed with the teachings of the Bible.

Campbell was generally a strict, cold rationalist. In 1847, he made a trip to Ireland to deliver funds to help those experiencing the Great Famine and then toured England and Scotland giving public lectures. In Glasgow, he was challenged by James Robertson to a debate about slavery in America. Campbell defended slavery as legal and not prohibited by the Bible. The exchange during the debate was fierce, and afterward Robertson sued Campbell for libel. Campbell was arrested and imprisoned for 10 days. The case was tried, and the jury found Campbell not guilty.

In Douglas Foster's book, *A Life of Alexander Campbell* he says the following regarding his underlying belief in white supremacy:

> *"Campbell's deeply held notions of white supremacy emerged in the articles in many ways. This was not simply a matter concerning a problematic political or social institution, he insisted. It was about the complete inconceivability that blacks and whites could ever live together in a relationship of equality. Campbell attacked abolitionists for having a philosophy completely out of harmony with the genius of human nature. 'There may be black States and white States, as there are red men and white men. But there shall never be, on Abolition principles, an abolition of slavery in the midst of a white population."*[20]

Campbell cast a huge shadow over the Restoration movement that influenced my family's heritage for generations. At the end of his biography of Alexander Campbell, Douglas Foster offers these concluding thoughts:

> *"He left a movement with a zeal for Scripture—for restoring the ancient gospel, order and unity of the primitive church. He left a body committed to intellectual excellence and simple participatory worship, and to evangelism and international missions that would take his cause to most nations of the world by the twenty-first century.*
>
> *However, he also left behind a movement that embraced, as did he, the myth of white supremacy embedded in the ethos of the United States yet so contrary to the message of Christ. His North American descendants, with few exceptions, defended segregation and subordination of persons of color during the nineteenth and twentieth*

centuries, and the churches today remain predominately white. The number of black congregations is fewer than 10 percent, and creating truly multiracial congregations has been a struggle."

A few leaders in the Restoration Movement were clear and outspoken Abolitionists. In 1841, Jonas Hartzel, who was from Ohio, published a tract entitled *The Sin of Slavery* that was mailed to many people who subscribed to *The Millennial Harbinger*. It appealed to the statement of Jesus that a man should treat his neighbor as he would treat himself. Hartzel also appealed to the Golden Rule in Luke 6:31: in essence, "Do to others as you would have them do to you." His argument to slaveowners was they in turn should be willing to be subject as a slave to a Black man and undergo the same suffering he endured. Abolitionists also argued it was against the law of God for a master to rob his slave of his earnings. (Matthew 25 :45) "*...whatever you did not do for one of the least of these, you did not do for me."* A preacher named Pardee Butler pointed out it was a sin to sell human beings and separate them from family and friends.[21]

In 1855, an article in *North-Western Christian Magazine* said Restoration churches should not have fellowship with slaveowners and with those who would not condemn slavery. Alexander Campbell printed a response expressing sorrow over their position.

In addition, a few people in the Restoration Movement openly promoted a proslavery view. In 1849, James Shannon wrote he believed slavery was approved in the Bible. He cited the obscure story of the "Curse of Ham and his son Canaan" referred to in Genesis 9:25-27.

A majority of the members of the Restoration churches did not want to divide the pursuit of restoring the First Century church over trying to resolve the issue of slavery. Slavery was a matter of opinion—a "political issue." However, this so-called middle view evolved into radical attitudes of sectionalism and nationalism, leading to the horrors of the Civil War. This resulted in many men from these churches in combat against each other in a war costing more than 600,000 lives.

Frederick Douglass (1817–1895) was born a slave and escaped to the North at the age of 20. He was a national leader of the abolitionist movement in America and one of the most significant orators and writers of his time. He was a contemporary to both Barton W. Stone and Alexander Campbell and was himself a convert to Christianity. In the appendix of his book *Narrative of the Life of Frederick Douglass, an American Slave* he called out the hypocrisy of slave-owning Christians:

> *"What I have said respecting and against religion, I mean strictly to apply to the slaveholding religion this land, and with no possible reference to Christianity proper; for, between the Christianity of this land, and the Christianity of Christ, I recognize the widest possible difference—so wide, that to receive the one as good, pure, and holy, is of necessity to reject the other as bad, corrupt, and wicked. To be the friend of one, is of necessity to be the enemy of the other. I love the pure, peaceable, and impartial Christianity of Christ: I therefore hate the corrupt, slaveholding, women-whipping, cradle plundering, partial and hypocritical Christianity of this land."*[22]

The Restoration Movement churches were complicit in slavery and hid behind a moderate or middle view that the right to own (as property) other image bearers of the Creator as a mere political question to be resolved by secular men. This at best passive view held by Churches of Christ persisted long after the Civil War. In 1963, Dr. Martin Luther King, Jr., called out the white moderate Christians in his "Letter from Birmingham Jail":

> *"I must make two honest confessions to you, my Christian and Jewish brothers. First, I must confess that over the past few years I have been gravely disappointed by the white moderate. I have almost reached the regrettable conclusion that the Negro's great stumbling block in his stride toward freedom is not the White Citizen's Counciler or the Ku Klux Klanner, but the white moderate, who is more devoted to order than justice; who constantly says: 'I agree with the goal you seek, but cannot agree with your methods of direct action,' who*

paternalistically believes he can set the timetable for another man's freedom; who lives by a mythical concept of time and who constantly advises the Negro to wait for a 'more convenient season.' Shallow understanding from people of good will is more frustrating than absolute misunderstanding from people of ill will. Lukewarm acceptance is much more bewildering than outright rejection.

...I must honestly reiterate that I have been disappointed with the church. I do not say this as one of those negative critics who can always find something wrong with the church. I say this as a minister of the gospel, who loves the church; who was nurtured in its bosom; who has been sustained by its spiritual blessings and who will remain true to it as long as the cord of life shall lengthen.

...In the midst of a mighty struggle to rid our nation of racial and economic injustice, I have heard many ministers say: 'These are social issues, which the gospel has no concern.'

The Restoration Churches and their leaders were focused on going back to the Bible to get church organization and worship practices right at the expense of caring for the plight of Black Americans, including those who were followers of Christ.

The history of the Churches of Christ is in my DNA. It made a deep impression on my personality and world view. Much of that influence has been for good and a true blessing I am thankful for each day. However, there are flaws in that history I should not run away from, and I should confess had negative effects on how I think, both consciously and subconsciously. Studying our history can be inspiring and humbling.

"History is not a random sequence of unrelated events. Everything affects, and is affected by, everything else. This is never clear in the present. Only time can sort out events. It is then, in perspective, that patterns emerge."...William Manchester[23]

Many people would say that the "golden age" of the Churches of Christ was from the 1920s to the 1970s. Nostalgia is a dangerous mindset, romanticizing the past and discouraging any rational study of history. One of my favorite comedy bits is by Seth Myers on his television show *Late Night with Seth Myers*. The bit is called "Back in My Day." Myers puts on an old sweater and sits in a high-backed chair and pretends to be smoking a pipe as he sarcastically reminisces about how life was simpler and better back in the "good 'ole days." A version I might do would be:

> *"Back in my day... I remember when the church didn't need youth*
> *ministers or youth groups...we just hung around on the church lawn*
> *after services and were entertained as we watched the deacons smoke*
> *a cigarette on the church porch—because your body was a temple*
> *that enjoyed nicotine."*

In the perceived "golden age," the white Churches of Christ did not experience the marginalization Dr. King spoke of in his letter. They look back at the past through the blurry lens of nostalgia.

When I study the history of racism in the United States, my own family, and my own church, I see how my view of the world has been filtered by the lens of white centeredness. Just because I never owned a slave does not mean I am not connected to the sins of our culture's past and that I do not need to confess and repent. I was significantly influenced for good by those church leaders who probably included my ancestors at the "unity" meeting on December 31, 1831. However, I cannot deny I grew up in a heritage of slaveholding and white centeredness—but somehow, I did not absorb some of that heritage...whether it be bias or prejudices I am not aware of or have rationalized. [24]

Obviously, I benefit from historical privileges given to white people. It's not a good feeling, but as a Christian, it calls me to confession and repentance. From the Book of Common Prayer:

> *The Deacon or Celebrant says.*
> Let us confess our sins against God and our neighbor.
> *Minister and People*
> Most merciful God,
> we confess that we have sinned against you

In thought word and deed,

by what we have done,

and by what we have left undone.

We have not loved you with our whole heart;

we have not loved our neighbors as ourselves.

We are truly sorry and we humbly repent.

For the sake of your Son Jesus Christ,

have mercy on us and forgive us;

that we may delight in your will,

and walk in your ways,

to the glory of your Name. Amen[25]

Chapter 7

JOHN B. FLOYD—IN THE NEWS

Historical Marker
Restland Cemetery, Dallas, Texas

According to family lore I heard growing up in Richardson, my third great-grandfather, John B. Floyd, was a pioneer who moved to Texas from Kentucky in 1855. He bought 900 acres in Dallas County, today occupied by Texas Instruments and Restland Cemetery. He and his family built the first two-story house in Dallas County and ran it as a famous stagecoach inn. He also was a Christian who gave the land for the Church of Christ in Richardson and was a founding trustee of that congregation in 1874. He was known to have a political background and served as a member of the Kentucky State Legislature. Family lore also held that he brought enslaved African Americans from Kentucky to Texas, but that they were "happy" with the situation of being enslaved and that they even decided to stay with the "benevolent" Floyds when they were later offered their freedom.

I always wondered if there were more discoverable details to this story, especially since John B. Floyd seemed to be a significant figure in the history of north Dallas County. I wondered about records of enslaved people being emancipated. So, in late 2021, I engaged some researchers with "ancestryPro-Genealogists" to research his history as a politician, church planter, and slaveowner. This proved to be very enlightening and provided a much different narrative regarding John B. Floyd's view of slavery. The research of the U.S. Federal Census, county records, and *Newspapers.com* revealed a different story. The following newspaper articles were found:

- "Jackson Convention," *Frankfort Argus*, Frankfort, Kentucky, December 15, 1830

- "Jackson Convention," *Frankfort Argus*, Frankfort, Kentucky, January 11, 1832

- "More Fugitives," *Louisville Daily Courier*, Louisville, Kentucky, June 22, 1855

- "Political Meeting in Dallas," *Dallas Daily Herald*, Dallas, Texas, February 15, 1860

- "Public Meeting in Collin County," *Dallas Daily Herald*, Dallas, Texas, June 13, 1860

- "Untitled (Candidate for state senate)," *Dallas Daily Herald*, Dallas, Texas, July 3, 1861

- "Mass Meeting in Dallas," *Dallas Daily Herald*, Dallas, Texas, January 12, 1865

- "Co-operation Meeting," *Dallas Daily Herald*, Dallas, Texas, September 4, 1869

- "Exciting Chase of a Thief," *Dallas Daily Herald*, Dallas, Texas, March 26, 1870

These articles provide significant information about Floyd and insight into his thinking regarding enslaving people and a brief picture of his role in Churches of Christ located in North Texas.

John B. Floyd was the son of David Floyd, born in Fauquier, Virginia, between 1771 and 1775 (based upon the 1820 and 1830 censuses). John was the son of David's first wife Catherine Burdett, and David lived in Gallatin County, Kentucky as early as 1820. Gallatin County was later divided to create three additional counties, including Trimble County where the Floyds lived. Trimble County is located approximately 40 miles northeast of Louisville, Kentucky and its north boundary is the Ohio River and the state of Indiana.

Research done by Ancestry.com revealed that David Floyd had three enslaved people in 1820 per the Federal Census:

Age	Males	Females
Under 14 years	1	
14-25 years		1
23-44 years	1	

The Federal Census of 1830 showed that David Floyd had nine enslaved people:

Age	Males	Females
Under 10 years	2	2
10-23 years	2	
24-35 years		1
36-54 years	1	1

David Floyd's will was "proved" in June of 1840, which would indicate he died probably in the latter half of 1839. The "Inventory of the Estate," dated June 20, 1840, listed the following enslaved people:

- "One yellow boy named Frances"
- "One black boy named Moses"
- "One black boy named Rueben"
- "One black girl named Sarah"

David Floyd's Will Book, dated November 29, 1829, includes provisions that his daughter, Ann, at his death "shall take for part of her legacy my negro girl, Sarah, and one of my negro boys Stephen or Moses should they be living at my death." In addition, he says "that my wife Esther have my negro man Reuben at my death should the privileges above allotted to her be deemed not sufficient for her support." It does not appear that John B. Floyd inherited any enslaved people from his father's estate.

Now, I want to look at the record of the enslaved people that were owned by John B. Floyd.

Research done by Ancestry.com revealed that John B. Floyd had four enslaved people in 1850 per the Federal Census:

- Female age 75 years
- Male age 20 years
- Female aged 18 years (possibly named Adaline)
- Male aged 18 years

On June 22, 1855, the following report was in the *Louisville Daily Courier*:

> *More Fugitives—Three negroes, belonging to John B. Floyd, of Trimble County, sloped for Canada on Sunday night—a man, a woman, and a child.*

Enslaved people in Kentucky were subject to strict laws limiting their movement away from their residences. They had to have a written pass if they were going to be away more than four hours and could not go more than eight to ten miles from their home. Those planning escapes would usually try to escape on Saturday or Sunday nights when they were not required to be at work. The fear of being "sold down the river" to the south or a sale that would break up a family would often prompt them to head north. Trimble County is just a few miles from the Ohio river and the state of Indiana. It is interesting to note that John Floyd was in Dallas County in June of 1855 when he bought land and began the plan to move to Texas. It seems highly likely that the enslaved man and woman were fearful of being put on the auction block for sale or fearful that the treatment in Texas could be harsher.

The Federal Census of 1860 showed that John B. Floyd had five enslaved people:

- Female age 30 (possibly named Adaline)
- Male age 26
- Male age 7 (possibly named Ephriam)
- Male age 3
- Male age 1 month

The Federal Census of 1870 showed that John B. Floyd's household included four "domestic servants and farm workers":

- Adaline Floyd, age 40, Back
- Ephriam Floyd, age 16, Black
- Luticia Floyd, age 8, Black
- Elize Floyd, age 7 Black

Note that the Black "domestic servants" listed in John Floyd's family were likely former enslaved people "belonging" to John before emancipation after the Civil War. The family lore was that these enslaved people were happy being slaves and remained with the Floyds even though they had been freed. The part of the story does not hold up. They were emancipated because the South lost the Civil War. It would be very difficult for Adaline, a single 40-year-old Black woman, to earn any kind of sustainable living for herself in 1870. More than

90% of the enslaved population at that time was illiterate and had no financial resources. It seems that staying with the Floyds was the only practical choice she had at that time, or rather she had no choice at all.

The following newspaper report was found the spring of 2022 by the research group at ancestry.com. This was a front-page story in *The Dallas Daily Herald* on February 15, 1860. Sam Houston had recently been elected Governor of the State of Texas, and some of the leading citizens in Dallas County were upset and concerned with the contents of Houston's inauguration speech was not "pro-slavery" enough. So, a "Political Meeting" was held in Dallas with these citizens to produce a written statement voicing their concerns and political wishes. The elected chairman of that meeting was my third great grandfather, John B. Floyd. This is the newspaper article:

The Dallas Daily Herald

February 15, 1860

"Political Meeting in Dallas"

Pursuant to a notice published several days previous—a meeting was held in the Court House, at 3 P. M. on Saturday, the 11th last.

On motion, John B. Floyd was called to preside, and J. M. Crockett requested to act as Secretary.

The President explained the object of the meeting, in a distinct and forcible manner. He had voted for Houston, for Governor, as many others had, believing him most suitable for the position, of the two candidates presented. He was dissatisfied with the opinions expressed in his inaugural and other documents published since his elections, upon the position of the North and the South; and as that dissatisfaction seems to be the common expression of these placed in like position with himself, he desired that, without distinction of party, we might give a public demonstration of the true sentiments of the citizens of Dallas county, not only on the course of General Houston, but also upon the aspect of our affairs in Congress, growing out of slavery agitation. He announced the meeting prepared to hear any motion or resolution, whereupon.

On motion of L. H. Pennington, a committee of four persons was appointed to draft suitable resolutions, to wit: Charles R. Pryor, A. A. Johnson, J. J. Good and F. M. Wiggington

On motion of Charles H. Pryor, Mr. Bruton was added to the committee.

B. H. Landay was then invited to take the Chair during the absence of the President and the committee retired.

The Chairman was vociferously called for and responded in his usual happy manner but declined to make a speech.

"McCoy! McCoy!" then resounded from every part of the room, amid a din of enthusiastic applause and he came, but not to make a speech. He did not fairly understand the object of the meeting. If there were those present who like the President of the meeting, desired to confess their political sins, let them do so. He had none to atone for. He had not voted for General Houston, and never expected to unless the preservation of Southern rights should demand it.

Col. Crockett was then called for, but did not respond. The Chairman remarked that it was the first time he had ever known that gentleman to refuse to a call of is fellow citizens.

Mr. Crockett said that he was prepared to discuss the subjects that might be presented by the resolutions, but before their introduction he was at a loss for a subject—would speak upon any subject that the meeting or Chairman would suggest. Urged to proceed—he was entering upon a view of the aspect of the political affairs of the General Government, when the committee returned.

The President resumed the Chair.

Judge Burford, having just entered for the purpose of discharging a jury, was chained to the spot by the overwhelming appeals of the *assembled citizens. When order was restored, the Judge informed the meeting that he would address then on the resolutions, when read.*

Gen. J. J. Good then proceeded to read the resolutions, in his usual clear and distinct style, as follows:

Resolved, 1st That slaves are recognized as property by the Constitution of the United States, and that Congress has no right to abolish it, or other species of property.

2d. That the Territories of the United States are the common property of the people of all the States, and until their organization as States, are held in trust by the United States for the benefit of the whole people; that Congress, having no authority to abolish slavery, or pass any law unfriendly to that institution, can delegate no such authority to the government of a Territory.

3d. That passing of such laws by the government of a Territory, would be a blow at the Constitutional rights of the South, and ought to be resisted by the people of the South, and all lovers of the Union.

4th. That any man or body of men who shall assert or contend that the Congress of the United States, or that the Legislature of any Territory under the jurisdiction thereof, has the right to abolish slavery, or to legislated against it in any way is untrue to the South, and an enemy to its interests.

5th. That the principles of the Republican party are unconstitutional, aggressive and sectional, and calculated to enslave the South, or drive then to desperate alternative of dissolution.

6th. That we regard the late election of Pennington as Speaker of the House, as one more step in the line of policy clearly marked out by the sectional Republican party, as leading to monopolize the offices and patronage of the General Government; and the consummation or success of such a policy would be disastrous to the South and the safety of the Union.

7th. That we look to the Charleston Convention, in the present distracted state of public sentiment, be the meeting of a conservative and national body, which we hope will aid in rendering peace and harmony.

8th. That we believe that it is the duty of all national and anti-sectional men, of whatever party, to cooperate and unite for the common safety and perpetuity of the Union.

9th. That we heartily endorse the doctrine of the reserved rights of the States, and will maintain those rights under any infractions of the Constitution, regarding our honor and rights as paramount to every other blessing that a free and independent people can enjoy.

10th. That we repudiate the sentiment enunciated by Governor Houston in his inaugural address to the Legislature of Texas, and in other documents, for using the following sentiment: "That the people of the South are equally guilty with the North, in regard to the agitation of the slavery question, together with the consequences growing out of the same," and that we disclaim the truth of such sentiment, in view of the fact that the fanaticism of the North on the subject of domestic slavery, has given just cause for whatever agitation exists among us.

11th. That, to secure union, the different counties of this State hold similar meetings, and give a firm expression of opinion upon the political questions now agitating the public mind.

John M. Crockett moved the adoption of the resolution, which was seconded by many voices. Mr. Crockett said he was prepared to address the meeting upon the resolutions, but would give way to Judge Burford, whom he desired to hear.

Judge Burford spoke about an hour and a half. His reasoning and illustrations were cogent and forgeable. He seemed to have attained his proper element. His manner was happy, his expressions confident, his positions bold. He was listened to, throughout with undimin-ished interest.

Mr. Crockett said he did not rise to make a speech, but to call for the question. The people had heard and understood the resolutions— they had been entertained by an able and eloquent address—they were impatient to give expression to their sentiments, and he asked that the question be now put.

"Question! Question!" enthusiastically arose from every quarter. The question—Shall the resolutions as read be adopted? —was announced The response was given without a dissenting voice.

A vote of thanks was tendered Judge Burford, for his able speech—a motion to publish the proceedings of the meeting and the resolutions, in the Dallas Herald, was adopted, and the meeting adjourned. J. B. FLOYD, President

Jno. M. Crockett, Secretary

This was shocking to me the first time I read it. How did my family not know this, or if they did, never discuss it? It does comply with a significant part of the family narrative: "you should know, Mark, that the Civil War was not fought over slavery; it was fought over "states' rights." Several of the resolutions in the statement talk about "states' rights." But it is obvious what they wanted Texas and the other states to have the right to do: the right to enslave Black people and own them into perpetuity.

The 9th resolution ends with this statement demonstrating a complete lack of self-awareness: "That ...regarding our honor and rights as paramount to every other blessing that a free and independent people can enjoy." From their position of "white supremacy," they have no regard that enslaved people should also be able to know the joy of being "free and independent."

Their repudiation in the 10th resolution of Houston's statement "that the people of the South are equally guilty with the North, in the agitation of the slavery question" is a staggering example of the self-righteous mindset of the South that still exists today.

John B. Floyd continued to be active on the political scene. In June 1860 he served on a special committee in Collin County, Texas, the county bordering Dallas County's north boundary. The following is the article in The Dallas Daily Herald that provides the details of this committee meeting:

The Dallas Daily Herald, June 13, 1860

Public Meeting in Collin County

Plano, Collin co., Texas, May 31, '60

A meeting of the citizens of Collin and Dallas counties being held in Plano, for the purpose of investigating a matter relative to the conduct, and certain language, which had been used by C. N. Drake, and S. A. Winslow, of Collin, with and to a certain Negro man, Dick, belonging to W. P. Martin, of Collin county, which had a tendency to mar the safety and peace of the neighborhood, and incite the slaves in our community to rebellion.

Mr. M. L. Huffman being called to the chair, briefly stated the design of coming together; after which, S. M. Wilkins and Capt. Beverly, were appointed assistant chairmen, and H. H. Gossom, Secretary.

Upon motion the meeting was then constituted a committee of the whole; witnesses were then called and examined relative to said conduct and language with said negro; which, after being fully discussed was submitted to a committee of the whole.

The chairmen then appointed to the following gentlemen a special committee to draft resolutions.

G. W. Barnett, Jas. C. Foreman, J. B. Floyd, J. C. Fain, Jno. Fain, W. G. Matthews, H. H. Gossom, W. N. Bush, Rob't Rowland, W. B. Blalack, Wm. McCamy and Wm. Hughes,

The meeting then adjourned for half an hour.

The special committee appointed Wm. McCamy chairman and J. B. Floyd secretary; after some deliberation the following resolutions were submitted.

Resolved, 1st That from the testimony adduced before this meeting, it is, in our judgement, expedient, for the safety and peace of this community, that C. N. Drake leave Collin county, on or before the 2d day of June next and continue his journey until he shall have passed the boundary of Texas, and never return within its limits.

2d. That it is the judgment of this meeting that S. A. Winslow leave Collin county, on or before the 1st day of July next and as soon as possible leave the State of Texas, and never return to said State.

Which were unanimously adopted by the committee of the whole; and on motion it was further

Resolved, That the chairman appoint a special committee of twelve to wait upon Mr. W. P. Martin, and request that he give his negro man Dick, fifty lashes well laid on, for certain misdemeanor; and if he refuse to do the same to perform said act themselves, and in the event said committee are forced to perform said whipping, we, the committee of the whole promise and agree to sustain any and all costs and damages in Court, should any arise hereafter against said committee in consequences of having performed said act, and that we subscribe our names hereunto in giving our votes for this resolution,

M. L. HUFMAN, T. A. DUNLAP,

G. W. BARNETT Wm. HUGHES

J. F. ROWLAND, J. H. KEARLEY

JNO. GRIDER of Dallas County

P. D. CRUME, JAS. C. FOREMAN,

JAS. C. FAIN, J. A. FAIN,

S. M. WILKINS, SANFORD BECK,

CAPT. BEVERLY, B. F. MATJHEWS,

C. W. BARNETT, H. H. GOSSOM,

of Collin County,

The chairman then appointed Mr. J. C. Foreman to select twelve persons including himself, to wait upon Mr. Martin, who selected the following gentlemen:

J. C. Foreman, Daniel Klepper, M. L. Huffman, Rob't Rowland, Parson Wilkins, Wm. Blalack, James C. Fain, B F. Matthews J. A. Fain, G. W. Matthews, Wm. Hughes, and Sanford Beck.

It was then resolved that these proceedings be published in the Dallas Herald, with the request that other papers copy. The meeting then adjourned.

M. L. HUFMAN,

S. M. WILKINS, Chairmen.

CAPT. BEVERLEY.

H. H. Gossom, Secretary

In this article, we see John B. Floyd serving as secretary of a committee investigating an incident described as *"conduct and certain language"* that *"had a tendency to mar the safety and peace of the neighborhood and incite the slaves in our community to rebellion."* The conversation was between an African American enslaved person named Dick and two other residents of Collin County named C. N. Drake and S. A. Winslow. The meeting is described as a "committee" of citizens of Collin and Dallas counties. It does not appear that this is a hearing held by the traditional judicial system of Collin County and does not have any legal authority. However, they seem more than comfortable in having the proceedings published *"in the Dallas Herald, with the request that other papers copy."* They called witnesses who were examined relative to the conduct of the African American called Dick. It does not indicate that Dick was there, or if any defense was provided for him. John B. Floyd was Secretary of a special sub-committee to draft a series of "resolutions" that were to be carried out. The committee asked that C. N. Drake and S. A. Winslow leave the state of Texas almost immediately. I found a notice in The Dallas Daily Herald, dated April 20,1859, listing individuals who registered at the St. Nicholas Hotel for various dates in April of 1859. It includes a listing of a S. A. Winslow who registered on April 13th, and he was from New York. I also found a September 27, 1861, notice in the *Buffalo Commercial* (New York) of a S. A. Winslow being chosen as a director of the Sandusky, Dayton, and Cincinnati Railroad Company and he is shown to be from Urbana. I then found a January 26, 1855, article in the *Urbana Citizen and Gazette* that listed S. A. Winslow as a named member of a law firm. My guess is that S. A. Winslow was a lawyer who might have been an abolitionist. I could not find any information on C. N. Drake.

The committee passes resolutions stating that Drake and Winslow leave Collin County on June 2nd and July 1st respectively and then proceed to leave the State of Texas. Then they pass a resolution that W. P. Martin, who owns Dick, to give Dick fifty lashes, "well laid on" for a "certain misdemeanor". They use the legal term misdemeanor as if they are judge and jury, but this appears to be several white guys taking justice into their own hands. The committee seems to have a concern as to whether Mr. Martin will carry out giving the fifty lashes to Dick. So, remarkably, they appoint another special committee of to do the "whipping" themselves if Mr. Martin does not. In addition, the "committee of the whole" agree to pay all costs and damages that the twelve special committees might incur if a future court of law finding this act illegal. This is a classic case of a white supremacy group taking the law into their own hands and is a precursor to what happened in the Jim Crow era and is happening even to this day.

So, sadly, Dick received fifty lashes for not being a "happy slave".

Apparently, John B. Floyd was a well-known political figure in North Texas, and he aspired to take his views to the Texas Legislature. The Following "Untiled" article appeared in the *Dallas Daily Herald* in July of 1861:

The Dallas Daily Herald

July 3, 1861

See announcement of John B. Floyd Esq., as a candidate for the Senate, in the Senatorial District composed of the counties of Dallas, Kaufman and Henderson. Mr. Floyd is well known to all as a good citizen, a sound politician of the session order, and every worthy of the consideration of his fellow citizens. He held high position in Kentucky previous to his immigration to Texas, having served in the Legislature of that state from Trimble County, and filled other local offices.

The Kaufman Democrat will please copy his announcement.

There are no records of John B. winning that election or ever serving in the Senate, but he certainly appears to be active in Texas politics. This is the first time the title of esquire appears after his name, indicating he is a lawyer. However, the formality of the writing found in the resolutions submitted by the political committees he served on certainly indicates a lawyer was involved in drafting them.

It is interesting the announcement states he is a politician of the "session order" since Texas had already seceded from the Union in February of 1861. However, the minutes from the political meeting in Dallas held in early 1860 leave no doubt he would favor succession from the Union.

In early January of 1965 leaders in Dallas County held a "mass meeting" to discuss the Civil War and slavery. John B. Floyd appears again as part of this meeting reported in the *Dallas Daily Herald* on January 12, 1865. The following is the news article:

The Dallas Daily Herald

January 12, 1865

"Mass Meeting in Dallas"

Dallas, Texas, January 7th, 1865

In pursuance of public notice, a very large number of the citizens of the county assembled at the Courthouse and upon being called to order, Col. N. H. Darnell, was called to preside and John W. Lane, was appointed Secretary. The chairman explained in a few remarks the object of the meeting to be to get an expression of the people upon the state of the country.

Col. Burford was invited to address the citizens, and did so in his usual forcible style, giving a brief history of the war, and very pertinently alluded to the utter impossibility of peace upon reconstruction.

On motion, Col. J. C. McCoy, Dr. H. J. Moffett, Col. J. V. Cockrell, Capt. James Thomas, R. M. Hawpe, Esq., Martin Riggs, Esq., and John B. Floyd, were appointed a committee to draft a preamble and resolutions, expressive of the sense of the meeting.

The meeting was then addressed in a forcible and pathetic manner by Col. Cockrell.

The committee after a short retirement returned and submitted the following report:

The committee appointed to draft a preamble and resolutions, expressive of the object of the meeting, and the sentiments of the people of Dallas county, Texas, upon the state of the country, ask leave to report the following, to-wit:

WHEREAS, the recent re-election of Abraham Lincoln by the Black Republicans of the North, to the Presidency of the United States, sufficiently serves to show to us, that we may expect a continuance of the policy pursued by that government towards us for the last four years, and admonishes us in advance that we may export the present war to be waged against us by that government, with as much or greater ruthlessness and barbarity as heretofore, and in total utter disregard of all human rules of civilized warfare, and

WHEREAS, the despot who imperiously rules the destinies of the North, has manifested by his various proclamations and messages, a settled hatred to the people of the South, and their institutions, and a disposition to heap insult and outrage, and

WHEREAS, this course of conduct serves only to strengthen us in our determination to resist to the death, and to make our separation from that government final, and our independence sure, therefore, be it

Resolved, 1st, That the war now being waged against the people of the South, and against their property and institutions by the United States government is wanton, unprovoked, cruel, unholy and unjust, and being conducted in violation of every principle which should govern, regulate and control civilized warfare. That our often repeated purpose never to submit to Yankee abolition rule and power, remains inflexible and unshaken; that our determination to remain free and independent, remains the same as when our first brave soldier offered himself a sacrifice on his country's altar' that it is our unalterable determination to make our separation from the government of the United States, permanent and final: that we desire Peace, with all its accompanying blessings, but that while such is our desire, we can only accept the same upon honorable terms and upon a basis of full recognition of our Independence, on the part of the United States Government.

Resolved, 2nd, That it is the paramount duty of every citizen of the South to sustain, invigorate, and assist in rendering effective one brave armies in the field to the full extent of his ability, and to furnish subsistence and necessaries, to the families of soldiers in the army, at prices corresponding to their means.

Resolved, 3d, That the brilliant achievements and successes of our arms, are such as to give hopeful assurances for the future dispelling the gloom from every brow, and cheering every heart.

Resolved, 4th, That relying upon the ability of the Executive, the skill of those who lead our armies, and the strong arms and stout hearts of our brave soldiers, the self-sacrificing devotion of our heroic women, the patriotism of our men, the justice of our cause, and above all the blessing of God who rules our distinies, we confidently abide the result.

Resolved, 5th, That we heartily approve the action of the Legislature of the State of Texas, at it last session, in passing a certain joint Resolution, entitled, "Joint Resolutions concerning Peace, Reconstruction and Independence", (hereto attached.) and that we endorse the sentiments therein contained to the fullest extent.

Resolved, 6th, That the "Dallas Herald," "State Gazette," and other papers throughout the State, be required to publish.

Committee,

> *J. C. McCOY*
>
> *JNO. B. FLOYD*
>
> *JAS THOMAS*
>
> *R. M. HAWPF*
>
> *MARTIN RIGGS*
>
> *H. J. MOFFEIT*
>
> *J. V. COCKRELL*

Joint Resolutions Concerning Peace, Reconstruction and Independence.

WHEREAS, among the political parties in the United States the question of a re-union of these States with those of the Confederacy is being agitated, and in order to promote such re-union it is urged that delegates be chosen from each of the States in the Confederacy and in the Union, to meet in Convention to reform the Constitution of the United States which proposition is coupled with the quasi pledge that such amendment shall be made to the Constitution as will forever guarantee the institution of African slavery in the States of this Confederacy.

AND, WHEREAS, it is possible that the political party in the United States advocating that proposition may prevail at the approaching election in choosing the Executive of that Government, and that consequentially the foregoing proposition may be attempted to be made to the States of the Confederacy; Now, we of the State of Texas, believing that it is proper to meet such proposition in advance, have resolved as follows:

Resolution 1st. Be it resolved by the Legislature of the State of Texas, That neither the above proposition or any other can be made to the people of this State, by the United States or any other foreign people, the Government of the Confederate States being the only organ of the States in the Confederacy, for the transaction of business with foreign nations, and such proposition, if made at all, must be made to the Confederate States, and, if made to this State, will not be entertained.

Resolution 2d. That we recognize in that proposition no good faith, but merely an insidious policy, to "divide and conquer;" a policy through which it is hoped to detach some of the States from the Confederacy, thereby to weaken and demoralize the rest. To accomplish this an appeal is made to our love of property, which, as it is the all-prevailing motive to the actions of the people of the North, they supposed would control our conduct.

Resolution 3d. That it will be well for the people of the North to understand, even at this late day, that the Southern States did not secede from the Union upon any question such as the mere preservation the slave property of their citizens; but, being free sovereign States, they were resolved to preserve their freedom and their sovereignty. They were free to govern themselves as they, not others, saw fit. They were free to change their government, to erect a new one and to make whatever alliances they should choose. And after nearly four years of arduous war, these States are still unwavering in their resolution to preserve their freedom and their sovereignty, without which all else is valueless.

Resolution 4th. That could the present war, and all its horrors be blotted our of our memories, our past experience while in the Union would warn us from any re-union with the people of the North. A written Constitution adopted by our ancestors and theirs, which contained plainly worded guarantees of the rights of all, was by them and their sworn representatives deliberately and persistently violated to our injury and finally, after years of discussion, when the question was understandingly before the people at large, they elected a Chief Magistrate with the purpose that he should destroy our liberties, in disregard of the Constitution which he had sworn to support; thus exhibiting an instance of radical and wide-spread national depravity, to the honor of human nature, never exhibited in the world before.

Resolution 5th. But we could not if we would, banish from our memory the inhumanities of this war. Our enemies have repudiated every principle of civilized warfare. They have withdrawn their felons from Jails and Penitentiaries, have recruited from the scum of Europe, armed our slaves, in order to procure an army sufficiently atrocious for their purpose; and this army has been launched upon us with the declared object of our extermination. Poisoned weapons have been manufactured and used. Exchange of prisoners has been refused until the success of our armies extorted a cartel and the terms of this have been violated by them whenever the varying fortune of the field made it apparently advantageous to do so. Our countrymen when captured have been removed to rigorous climes, and subjected to every hardship, that they thus might be destroyed. Non-combatants have been murdered. Indiscriminate onslaught has been made upon tottering age and tender youth. Our chaste and defenseless women have been submitted to outrage worse than death. Peaceful villages have been bombarded, and happy homes plundered and burnt. Whole populations have been removed and bondaged to Northern masters. Desolation has marched with their armies. Religious services have been prohibited; ministers of the gospel of peace have been incarcerated and silenced, and sacrilegious hands have been laid upon our sacred altars. Lying to themselves that they are fighting the battle of freedom for four millions of happy and contented negroes, they are attempting the enslavement of eight millions of freemen. With devilish mockery of philanthropy, they have deluded and dragged these negroes from their comfortable homes to use them as screens from our weapons in the day of battle, and they have sent them by thousands to painful death by neglect, exposure and starvation. Words cannot express the malignity in their hearts or the atrocity of their deeds, exceeding as they do all that was ever conceived by men, from the Scythian down to the Comanche. Nor has this been the conduct of an unbridled soldiery merely. Those officers of the army who have surpassed the rest of the infamous in infamy, have been rewarded with promotion by their Government. Nor has their Government been alone in identifying itself with these crimes. The people of the North have never failed, when given the opportunity was presented to render ovations to the most transcendent among the criminals, while their press has been constant in its laudation, and their orators and preachers have cried out, "well done." Army, Government and people, have united to *make the name of Yankee, suggestive as it was before of fraud, now the synonym of barbarism and baseness.*

Resolution, 6th, By the just pride of the manhood and the virtue which we can claim as individuals and as a people, by the divine command which warns us not to walk in the way with the wicked; by the memory of our murdered dead; by the sight of the bereaved mothers, widows, sisters, daughters and orphans in our land; by the heart-brokenness of trampled virtue; and by our desolated hearth, we are forbidden to admit a thought of further association with the people of the North. Our heroic soldiers, the living, and the martyred dead, forbid it; and our trust in God forbids it.

Resolution 7th. We declare that we are earnestly desirous of peace, but we say no less distinctly that it must be coupled with our independence. And if the people of the United States be really disposed to terminate the war, they will best prove that disposition by making their propositions to the Government of the Confederate States which alone can entertain it.

Resolution 8th, That a copy of these resolutions be transmitted to the President of the Confederate States to each of our Senators and Representatives in Congress and to the Gov. of each State in the Confederacy.

On the presentation of the Preamble and Resolutions the meeting was addressed by Dr. Moffett, in their behalf, and urging concert of action and harmony of feeling in this struggle for liberty.

On motion the Preamble and Resolutions were unanimously adopted.

On motion the meeting adjourned sine die.

N. H. DARNELL, Chairman

Jon W. Lane, Secretary

John B. Floyd served on the committee appointed to draft the preamble and resolutions of this document. I have highlighted some of the contents in the bullet points below:

- The recent "re-election of Abraham Lincoln by the "Black Republicans of the North" meant a continuation of the War
- Lincoln was a "despot who imperiously rules the destinies of the North"
- "Our determination to resist to the death" to separate from the US government
- The Constitution of the United States should be amended that would "forever guarantee the institution of African Slavery in the States of this Confederacy"
- Then a conflicting statement was made that "the Southern States did not secede from the Union upon any question such as the mere preservation the slave property of their citizens"
- Our enemies...have armed our slaves
- "Lying to themselves that they are fighting the battle of freedom four million of happy contented negroes...With devilish mockery of philanthropy, they have deluded and dragged negroes from their comfortable homes to use them as screens from our weapons in the day of battle"
- The North is "attempting the slavery of eight million of freeman"

These statements are so problematic and sad. John B. Floyd and his fellow Texans were willing to fight a war resulting in the deaths of more than 600,000 people in order to forever have the right to enslave African Americans. They deride the bravery of the approximately 200,000 Black soldiers who served in the Union army to fight for their freedom by referring them to as "screens from our weapons." And they maintain the "happy slave" myth and make the ridiculous reference to the "comfortable homes" of the enslaved. However, in just three months on April 9, 1865, General Robert E. Lee would surrender to Ulysses S Grant at Appomattox, Virginia. The Civil War would come to an end, and Texas would rejoin the Union.

John B. Floyd was a member of the Church of Christ when he lived in Trimble, County, Kentucky, where the Churches of Christ began. He was active in that church in North Texas. The next article found about him had to do with a meeting of leaders of Churches of Christ located in Dallas, Collin, and Kaufman counties. After the Civil War in 1869 we find John B. Floyd acting as the chairman of a meeting between leaders from Churches of Christ. The following article in the Dallas Daily Herald tells of a meeting of church leaders from Dallas, Collin and Kaufman counties:

Co-operation Meeting

The Dallas Daily Herald

September 4, 1869

At a cooperation meeting held at Spring Creek near Plano August 9, 1869,

(previous notice having been given by publication in the Dallas Herald) for the advancement of the cause of Christ's Kingdom in the counties of Collin, Dallas and Kaufman it was

Resolved, That we, as members of the Church of Christ and said counties do recommend a cooperation of all the congregations in said counties for the purpose of sending an Evangelist or Evangelists, whose business it shall be to visit each congregation in the above named district, and set the same in order where found necessary, to which end we invite each congregation to send representatives to a co-operation meeting to be held at Rockwell, Kaufman county, on the third Lord's d Day in October, 1869 with full instructions as to who the congregations they represent desire should serve them, together with the amount contributed for that purpose, said amount to be placed in the hands of a treasures selected by said meeting, to hold and pay the same over quarterly in advance to the Evangelist or Evangelists employed by the meeting, and should said meeting fail to employ an Evangelist, the money raised for that purpose shall be refunded to the parties contributing the same.

The congregations are also requested to send up by their representatives a statement showing the name of their preachers and officers, the number of members, times of meeting and general condition.

Resolved, That there be a financial committee, composed of Brothers S B M Fowler, V J Sterman, James L Floyd, G B Jacks, and Wm. Elkin whose duty it shall be to place two Evangelists in the field at once, to labor until the.

above-named meeting in October; also local committee consisting of brothers James Holland of Pleasant Valley, John Hampass, of Cedar Creek, A. B. Rawlins, of Lancaster, James Sheppard of Dallas, J. S. Mase, of McKinney, and Sims and King of Wells' Bridge whose duty it shall be to assist the former committee of raising means to support the said Evangelists.

Resolved, That a copy of these proceedings be furnished the Dallas Herald, Kaufman Statt, McKinney Enquirer, McKinney Messenger with request to publish.

JOHN B. FLOYD, Ch'n.

R. W. Carpenter, Sec'y

The writing in this article is very similar to other resolutions from meetings where John B. Floyd served as a secretary or committee member. They are structured like legal documents and identify John B. Floyd as a lawyer. John again appears in a leadership role in this effort to have Churches of Christ in this area of north Texas raise funds together to pay evangelists to visit congregations of Churches of Christ and "set the same in order where found necessary." This seems to indicate that the evangelists would determine if the churches they visited were in need of some corrective teaching to bring them under some type of perceived orthodoxy found in a true "Restoration Movement" church.

They also are requesting an accounting of the preachers, officers, members and "general condition." The financial committee of this "Co-operation Meeting" also included James L. Floyd, son of John B. Floyd, who also was one of the founding trustees of the Richardson Church of Christ.

It is interesting to note that this church "co-operation" is in stark contrast to my grandfather Walter Mackoy, who helped start an "anti-cooperation" Church of Christ in Grayson County, Texas, about 80 years later.

The last time John B. Floyd appears in the news is an article in the *Dallas Daily Herald* on March 26, 1870, entitled "Exciting Chase of a Thief." It's the story of a man named Camp who stole five horses in Collin County and on his way to Dallas one of the horses fell into a well near the stagecoach inn of John B. Floyd. The neighborhood helped retrieve the horse and Camp went on to Dallas where he swapped the horse for a younger one. He then returned to the Floyd stagecoach inn, where he spent the night. It is interesting to note that the article added the title of Esquire to John B. Floyd's name, again indicating he was a lawyer.

I never knew any details of John B. Floyd's political life until these news articles were found. I previously assumed he was just swept up in the culture of Kentucky and that the "peculiar institution" of slavery was not his first choice, especially since he was a Christian and an active supporter of local churches. However, the family story I was told has proved to be a romanticized myth hiding a lack of acknowledgement and confession of sin. In contrast, my third great-grandfather, Moses Mackoy, was also a participant in the "peculiar institution" of slavery found in Kentucky. But as a young man he seemed to have a different understanding that enslaving African Americans was not right. And so, he started a school to teach literacy to the enslaved. He at least saw some "gray areas." John B. Floyd was a hard-liner. He believed that the right to enslave people should go on forever. He saw no gray areas.

The Floyds were still influential in my becoming a follower of Jesus. My great-grandmother, Annie Artimesia Floyd, died a year before I was born in 1949. In last years of her life, she lived with her daughter, Winnie Saunders

Wallis, and her family in the house next to the house where I grew up. Winnie Wallis was a dedicated Christian and a key person in the Abrams Road Church of Christ that her grandfather, James L. Floyd along with John B. Floyd helped found. She was good, kind, and happy person—not what you would call a "hard-liner." By the way, she also would worry to the point of being ill when bad weather would be coming. She lost her father, Thomas Saunders when she was just 13 years old when he was injured in a farming accident that required, they amputate part of his leg on the kitchen table of their home. He then later died from an infection in that leg. Winnie lost her second daughter as a result of kidney disease when Mildred was just 22 years old. Like others of her generation, she lived through the first pandemic, the Great Depression, and two world wars. Life had not always been easy. But she was a Christian, she loved the local church, and she believed that when the church doors were open—you should be there. The only time she really ever got upset with me was when I was a freshman at Harding College. As a freshman at Harding, you had a one-hour Bible class five days of the week, chapel five days a week, and you went to church Sunday morning, Sunday night and Wednesday night. Also, on Sunday morning after the church service they had Sunday school class. I had made the bold decision to "skip" the Sunday school class. Granny Winnie got wind of my skipping. She let me know that she did not approve and that it concerned her. I did go to Sunday school class a few times after that—but the main thing I took away from her admonition was to always make church a priority.

My dad, William C. Wallis, Jr., would now and then talk briefly about how we were Floyds and descendants of early pioneers who helped build Dallas County, And then he would sometimes add the comment: "You know Mark… the Floyds owned slaves, but they were "happy slaves" …and the Civil War was not about slavery, it was about states' rights."

He did not make the comment intending to open the subject up for discussion. So, I would often reply, "You know, Dad, I would not have been a happy slave."

Chapter 8

THE GIANT OF THEM ALL

Texas, Our Texas

(Official State Song, adopted in 1929)

Texas, our Texas! All hail the mighty State!
Texas, our Texas! So wonderful so great!
Boldest and grandest, Withstanding ev'ry test;
O Empire wide and glorious, you stand supremely blest.
Chorus
God bless you Texas! And keep you brave and strong
That you may grow in power and worth,
Thro'out the ages long.
II
Texas, O Texas! Your freeborn single star, Sends out its radiance
to nations near and far.
Emblem of freedom! It sets our hearts aglow
With thoughts of San Jacinto and glorious Alamo.
Chorus

III

Texas, dear Texas! From tyrant grip now free,
Shines forth in splendor your star of destiny!
Mother of heroes! We come your children true,
Proclaiming our allegiance, our faith, our love for you.
Chorus

One of my all-time favorite movies is *Giant*, an epic 198-minute saga set in Texas spanning from the 1920s to the early 1950s.[26] It is based on the best-selling novel by Edna Ferber and tells the story of a cattle-ranching dynasty on the enormous 595,000-acre Reata Ranch. Rock Hudson stars Bick Benedict and Elizabeth Taylor as his wife, Leslie. It also stars James Dean, in his last role, as ranch hand Jett Rink, who lucks into a parcel of oil-rich land, becoming a tycoon overnight. The filmmakers use numerous wide-angle shots of the immense land of the Lone Star State— "Giant." The film deals with Bick's attitudes about race. At first, he is apathetic about the awful living conditions of the Mexican Americans who work on the Reata. Bick evolves during his life, experiencing reformation in his views regarding social justice. The movie ends with him in a physical fight with a racist diner owner who has refused service to Bick's Mexican American daughter-in-law and grandson. The movie ends as the men trade blows while "The Yellow Rose of Texas" plays on the jukebox. I still remember seeing that final scene in the movie theater as a boy of around seven years old. It was "woke" for 1957—and probably too woke for some Texas politicians today. I have watched it many times over the years and now am a proud owner of the new 4KUltraHD version released in 2022.

Giant was and is a metaphor of how Texans think so highly of their state. It's about ranching, oil, independence, and the pursuit of wealth. In school, my generation would sing the song "Texas Our Texas." Texas was "so wonderful" the "supremely blest." When I went to college in 1968, I had traveled no further than Carlsbad, New Mexico, to the west; a band trip to Monterrey, Mexico, to the south; Ardmore, Oklahoma, to the north; and Little Rock, Arkansas, to the east. In my small world, Texas, was clearly the best. (Although I must admit that I loved the trees and rivers flowing through Arkansas.) Dallas was a dynamic growing city. The Texas Longhorns won national championships in football. Texas had strong oil and real estate industries along with growing high-tech companies like Texas Instruments. In addition, it was in the "Bible Belt," with churches around every corner. I was also taught that an additional bonus was to be part of the South. We were Southerners, part of the old Confederacy, and we were made aware that we should generally be suspicious of "Yankees" (Northerners).

We were more than Southerners—we had the distinction of being part of the Southwest. While cotton was big in the early days of Texas, it was the booming oil industry along with the cowboy culture that made Texas theoretically superior to the "Old South." Dallas was a city with swagger and a sophisticated banking system that provided ties to New York. And Texas was big. You needed a big car with a big gas tank. My wife, Susan, drove a 1990 Chevrolet Suburban during her days of driving carpool. That vehicle was 18 ¼ feet long, 6 feet high, with a 35-gallon gas tank. It had a blue and gold custom paint job with three rows of seats that were covered with a luxurious gold velvet material. This was a prototypical car for Texas. We had a friend in Atlanta at the time who wanted to buy a Suburban, but they were not available in Georgia—she had to come to Dallas to purchase one. Susan used her Texas experience to arrange the transaction with a dealer in Garland. The Suburban was a "Giant" vehicle that was made to be driven in the Southwest—it was not really a fit for the genteel ways of the Old South.

My third great-grandfather, John B. Floyd, moved his family from Kentucky to Texas in 1855. When they arrived, Texas had only been part of the United States for 10 years. The area known as Texas had been governed by five different countries: France, Spain, Mexico, the Republic of Texas, and the United States of America. In 1861, Texas would secede from the United States and become part of the Confederate States of America. A hundred years later, a new theme park opened in Arlington named "Six Flags Over Texas" in tribute to unusual history of the governance of our state. In 1990, the theme park boasted the tallest wooden roller coaster in the world, aptly named "The

Giant." Six Flags had an area called "The Confederacy" where actors conducted Civil War battle reenactments, and the Confederate battle flag was flown over the crowds of park patrons. In the early 1990s the name changed from "The Confederacy" to "The Old South"—and the battle flags were removed. However, the Confederate Stars and Bars remained one of the six flags flying at the park entrance. In August 2017, the park replaced the original six flags with six American flags.

The new country of Mexico was formed in 1821 after the Mexican War of Independence ended Spanish colonial rule. The new Mexican government enacted the "General Colonization Law," which enabled all households regardless of race to claim land in Mexico, and Mexican law and policy generally discouraged the institution of slavery. The colonization law recognized slavery but forbade the slave trade and stated that slaves born in the Mexican empire should be free at the age of 14. A Texas state law in 1828 allowed "labor contracts" made in foreign countries. Most Black people who entered Texas were nominally servants under labor contracts—but practically they were still slaves. In 1829, the Mexican President Guerro issued a proclamation ending slavery throughout Mexico. However, Texans protested this. Guerro's decree was nullified with respect to Texas. However, an act of the Mexican legislature in 1832 barred the introduction of new slaves and those who were under "debt servitude" contracts were limited to 10 years.

Mexican laws and policy threatened the institution of slavery in Texas. In 1835, the year of the Texas Revolution, Stephen F. Austin wrote that "Texas must be a slave country. It is no longer a matter of doubt." Slavery may have not been the only reason for the Texas Revolution of 1835, but "Texas violations of Mexican law in regard to slavery" certainly was a major influence in the reason for revolt.

"John S. (Rip) Ford, physician, journalist, and hero of the early Texas Rangers, espoused slavery as a principle more hallowed and indispensable than the tenants of the Declaration of Independence. He said, 'The assumption of the Declaration of Independence that

'all men are created equal' was not intended to include the African race or was a falsehood on its face.' Ford also cited Christianity as moral underpinnings of slaveholding. "The Savior erected his standard in the very midst of bondsmen, and while rebuking every species of sin, never based his voice against the legitimacy of the institution."

—*Jim Scutze*[27]

Most of the people who immigrated to Texas were from Southern states. They brought their Southern values and their belief in the slavery of black people. The original Constitution of the Republic of Texas written in 1836 included these provisions that reflected those values:

- All persons of color who were slaves for life before their emigration to Texas, and who are now held in bondage, shall remain in the like state of servitude, provide the said slave shall be the bona fide property of the person so holding said slave as aforesaid.

- Congress shall pass no laws to prohibit emigrants from the United States of America from bringing their slaves into the Republic with them, and holding them by the same tenure by which such slaves were held in the United States; nor shall Congress have power to emancipate slaves; nor shall any slave-holder be allowed to emancipate his or her slave or slaves, without the consent of Congress, unless he or she shall send his or her slave or slaves without the limits of the Republic.

- No free person of African descent, either in whole or in part, shall be permitted to reside permanently in the Republic, without the consent of Congress, and the importation or admission of Africans or negroes into this Republic, excepting from the United States of America, is forever prohibited, and declared to be piracy.

- All persons, (Africans, the descendants of Africans, and Indians excepted,) who were residing in Texas on the day of the Declaration of Independence, shall be considered citizens of the Republic, and entitled to all the privileges of such.

In 1840, the Texas Congress adopted a law which required all free Black people to leave Texas by January 1, 1842. Republic of Texas President Sam Houston eventually postponed the date to 1845.

Texas was annexed by the United States in 1845, and a new state constitution was written and adopted that was approved towards the end of that year. Article VIII of that constitution provided for the institution of slavery to continue in Texas.

ARTICLE VIII.

Slaves.

SEC. 1. *The legislature shall have no power to pass laws for the emancipation of slaves without the consent of their owners, nor without paying their owners, previous to such emancipation, a full equivalent in money for the slaves so emancipated. They shall have no power to prevent emigrants to this State from bringing with them such persons as are deemed slaves by the laws of any of the United States, so long as any person of the same age or description shall be continued in slavery by the laws of this State: Provided, That such slave be the bona fide property of such emigrants: Provided, also, That laws shall be passed to inhibit the introduction into this State of slaves who have committed high crimes in other States or Territories. They shall have the right to pass laws to permit the owners of slaves to emancipate them, saving the rights of creditors, and preventing them from becoming a public charge. They shall have full power to pass laws which will oblige the owners of slaves to treat them with humanity; to provide for their necessary food and clothing; to abstain from all injuries to them, extending to life or limb; and, in case of their neglect or refusal to comply with the directions of such laws, to have such slave or slaves taken from such owner and sold for the benefit of such owner or owners. They may pass laws to prevent slaves from being brought into this State as merchandise only.*

SEC. 2. In the prosecution of slaves for crimes of a higher grade than petit larceny, the legislature shall have no power to deprive them of an impartial trial by a petit jury.

SEC. 3. Any person who shall maliciously dismember, or deprive a slave of life, shall suffer such punishment as would be inflicted in case the like offence had been committed upon a free white person, and on the like proof, except in case of insurrection by such slave.

As was true in the states of Virginia and Kentucky, slavery was not something that just evolved and happened because of some "natural process" that God intended. It was a cruel institution that was enthusiastically prosecuted and debated on the record by white people in the legislatures, constitutional conventions, and courts of Texas. There is a line in the song, "Texas, Our Texas" that says: "Texas, dear Texas! From tyrant grip now free." The "tyrant," Mexico, was against slavery. If you were a black person, then you were not free from the oppressor's grip.

Common Texas lore typically promotes a myth that slaves were treated better in Texas than they were in the South. Like Kentucky, the pitch would be—at least we're not Alabama or Mississippi. Rupert Richardson, former professor of history at Hardin-Simmons University, makes this ludicrous statement in his 1943 history book, "Texas—The Lone Star State," 5th edition:

"During the decade preceding the Civil War there was growing uneasiness about slavery in Texas. Vigilance committees became common. Slaves frequently ran away. Some renegades made their way into Mexico, others to the Indian Territory, and a few were arrested and returned. Apparently, most runaways returned voluntarily and were not severely punished...Slaves were well treated... They were permitted to earn a reasonable amount of spending money and they were rarely whipped. Evidence of the generosity of Texas masters is the complaint, frequently appearing in the press, that masters failed to discipline their slaves properly."[28]

Really? Really? I would like to ask Rupert, "When did you stop beating your wife?" He's really laying out a picture of "the American Dream" that was afforded to enslaved back people in Texas. Masters were generous because they were not disciplining their slaves enough. It was great to be "rarely whipped" and to have some spending money...even though you were not free to spend it how you wanted. And hey, how about those fun "vigilance committees"—you know, like the one John B. Floyd was on where they administered 50 lashes to a black enslaved person for even talking about more freedom. Really?

(Note: The quote above by Richardson does not appear in the current 11th edition of this book published in 2021.)

It does not appear that slaves were treated better in Texas than elsewhere and in some cases may have been treated worse. But all this rationalization that has been put forth as part of the "happy slave" myth that misses a big point... THEY WERE SLAVES!

From: "Black Texans—A History of African Americans in Texas, 1528-1995".[29]

Slave trade was done in markets in Galveston and Houston and enslaved families were often separated in this process. Masters would separate parents, brothers, and sisters, often to pay off their personal debts. The slaves worked as field hands on cotton, corn, and sugar plantations. They constructed roads, cut wood, built fences, handled livestock, dug wells and cleared land. A few enslaved were chosen as house servants—cooks, seamstresses, butlers, coachmen, nurses, etc. They generally worked Monday through Friday from 7:00 a.m. to 6:00 p.m. and half a day on Saturday. If owners had extra slaves, they would be hired out to others for $40 to $400 per year. Slave quarters in Texas usually were one- or two-room log cabins that were located near the main house of the slaveholder.

The enslaved could only expect lives where they repeated the same routine of hard work and minimal living conditions with no hope that these conditions would ever improve for their sons and daughters.

Slaveowners in Texas used various forms of punishment to control and create a subservient attitude towards them from their enslaved people. Most resorted to whipping but also employed the use of iron restraints, handcuffs, and sometimes jail. Dogs were used to pursue runaways, and some would allow the dogs to attack the fugitive. Enslaved people were not allowed to testify in court against slaveowners who mistreated them. Enslaved people were not allowed to sell agricultural products or hire their own time unless they were given special permission from their owners. As in Kentucky, they were required to have passes to leave their owners' properties, and counties had patrols to monitor slave movement and assemblies.

Most slaveowners brought their slaves to their churches and allowed them to sit in a segregated section of the building. Methodists, Baptists, Catholics, Episcopalians, Presbyterians, Christian Churches, and Churches of Christ all accepted enslaved members, while keeping the pews segregated. Churches generally taught that slavery was the normal state of the African American race. Many hoped that emphasis on the afterlife would ease the difficulties of living in slavery.

As in Kentucky, there was no legal basis for enslaved couples to marry, and it was up to owners to allow a formal marriage of an enslaved couple. All enslaved families faced the possibility of separation due to the possibility of the owner deciding to sell a family member. In addition, the freedom that some slaveowners exercised to have sexual relations with female slaves caused humiliation, bitterness, and sadness for slave women and their husbands.

Literacy schools for the enslaved were legal in Texas but only 5% of the slave population in Texas was literate at the end of the Civil War.

The Black enslaved individuals in Texas at this time had to learn how to survive and manage the general dispositions of hostility that their owners could have. They had to play the role of the "happy, docile, passive" slave. Also, a significant number of slaves ran away. Many sought freedom in Mexico. Martin Johnson, another former slave, made this comment regarding the "happy slave myth":

"Lots of old slaves closes the door before they tell the truth about slavery. When the door is open, they tell how kind their masters was and how rosy it all was. You can't blame them for this, because they had plenty of early discipline making then cautious about saying anything uncomplimentary about their masters. However, I can tell you the life of the average slave was not rosy. They were dealt plenty of cruel suffering."[30]

In the late 1850s, about 30% of Texans owned slaves but held 58% of the state's political posts. The slaveholders in Dallas grew insecure of their position at the end of the 1850s despite their political control. In January 1860, Charles Pryor, the editor of the *Dallas Herald* (the only weekly city newspaper) printed inflammatory articles telling of the evil work of abolitionist fanatics who might incite uprisings by slaves to harm whites. Fires and rumors of fires spread across the state in 1860. It is interesting to note that John B. Floyd was on a vigilante committee on June 13, 1860, that banished two white men from the state for promoting slave insurrection. All year long, Pryor had anticipated a racial conflict encouraged by Northern outsiders. On Sunday, July 8, 1860, between 1:00 and 2:00 p.m., a fire began in a rubbish heap outside the W. W. Peak and Brothers drugstore. It was 105 degrees that day and windy. The fire spread fast and reduced dry goods stores, law offices, groceries, inns, and the three-story Nicholas Hotel to ashes. The fire burned itself out and left the city in ruins. The next day, a 52-man "Committee of Vigilance" was formed and was presided over by District Judge Nat M. Burford. The committee met for 15 days and secretly interrogated almost 100 enslaved peoples and used torture tactics to extract confessions. The brutalized witnesses implicated all but three of the county's 1,074 slaves. Under Texas law, all of the accused would face the death penalty for insurrection and arson. The committee decided they could not afford to hang all the enslaved people, so they decided to execute three more prominent well-known enslaved people who had offended the "racial etiquette" of the day. Patrick Jennings because of an abrasive personality, Cato, who had a position of authority at the Overton mill, and Sam Smith who was a well-known enslaved preacher. The committee "symbolically" spared the life of a fourth enslaved person owned by W. B. Miller, but he was sent away from the area. Then the committee decided to whip every enslaved person in the county. *"We whipped every negro in the county one, by one"* —a source later told the *Dallas Morning News*. David Carey Nance recalled:

> *"Slaves being rounded by 'like cattle' and whipped 'without mercy'. Some slaves were almost beaten to death. The sight of the mass floggings, Nance later said, 'made his blood run cold"*...from *White Metropolis by Michael Phillips*

On July 24, 1860, the three accused enslaved people were hung on gallows on the bank of the Trinity River. This led to more violence in Texas, with mobs executing 80 slaves and 37 white abolitionists.

> *"One Mississippi newspaper editor sardonically described Texas slaves as "dancing to the music of cracking of the necks of the Abolitionists. This music, the Austin State Gazette predicted, would last until the final abolitionist was elevated on his platform."*
>
> — *"White Metropolis"* [31]

The general story of the experience of the enslaved in Texas has some similarity to those in Kentucky. However, Texas was not a Union border state and life was hard and brutal for the enslaved. It had formerly been an independent nation before it joined the United States and some saw Texas as possibly the last place where slavery could be maintained if the South lost the war. Texas could become an independent sovereign nation again and keep the peculiar institution. A former slave who made the journey from the Old South to Texas said that his master told him "In Texas there never be no freedom."

The writer Jim Schutz made this observation in 1986 in his book "The Accommodation":

> *"There is still in Dallas, and in much of Texas—especially among white people of a certain generation—an amount of self-delusion where the institution of Texas slavery is concerned. It is a popular belief that slavery was less harsh in Texas than in some parts of the*

Old South, even though every credible study of American slavery argues just the opposite. It is a popular white belief that, left to their own devices and without outside interference, white and Black Texans enjoy a special and friendly intimacy today, a legacy of their "partnership" in slavery, and, based on this deep bond and the essential nobility of the white Southern heart, a lasting racial peace could be attained, were it not for the meddling of outsiders who don't really "understand" that special relationship."[32]

I experienced this self-delusion firsthand growing up in Dallas County. I believe that as a sixth-generation Texan and native son of Dallas I can share inside observations I experienced in the Lone Star State. In addition, my wife Susan spent her key growing up years in Dallas. Susan is a stylish woman who understands the Dallas scene, but also possesses the down-to-earth quality of West Texas culture. We are both true Texans and have the accent to prove it. So, I want to share some of our experiences while living in the Dallas area and some of the history we experienced.

Leading Dallasites push the narrative that Dallas is a unique city with "no limits, no reason to be, and no history." The narrative has been that "Big D" is uniquely exceptional. I grew up with a vague narrative running in the back of my mind that there was a history of Dallas connected to my ancestors. The narrative was a simplistic tale of Christian pioneers who came to the fertile farmland of North Texas to pursue the Texan version of the American dream. However, in my gut, I always felt there had to be more to the story.

On the afternoon of November 22, 1963, I was walking down the hallway of Richardson Junior High School on the way to the band hall when I heard that President Kennedy had been shot. This was disturbing news and was difficult to absorb. My dad worked in Downtown Dallas and saw the President's motorcade go by just minutes before Kennedy, along with Texas governor John Connally, was shot in Dealey Plaza. It was a bizarre day. Oddly, I remember that, amid all the conversation at the dinner table that evening about what happened, my mother stopped and asked my dad if he was able to get a good look at Jackie Kennedy and if he could describe what she was wearing. Then on Sunday afternoon I was playing in our backyard when my parents were watching live coverage on TV, and they witnessed the accused assassin Lee Harvey Oswald being shot in the basement of the Dallas Police Headquarters. At that point, I remember spinning tops with my brother on our patio, wondering if we were living in a safe place. The Kennedy assassination put the city of Dallas on the map—but not in a good way. The mythical image of an "exceptional Dallas" was significantly fractured that day. Dallas was the setting of one our nation's darkest days. The previous criticisms made by outsiders had come to roost.

On November 20, 1960, I attended my first NFL game in the Cotton Bowl in Fair Park. The winless Dallas Cowboys were playing the San Francisco 49ers on a misty Sunday afternoon. It was the first season for the Cowboys, and there were probably 20,000 fans in the stadium that held around 75,000. It was an awesome experience for a 10 year old. I became a diehard Cowboy fan. In those days, my dad could buy one adult end-zone ticket and take five kids for free, and we did that several times. The Cowboys were coached by the now legendary Tom Landry, and they did not have a winning season until 1966, when they won the NFL East division and played the Green Bay Packers for the NFL Championship. Tom Landry went on to have 20 consecutive winning seasons that included five Super Bowl appearances with two of those being wins. During that era, the Dallas Cowboys became known as "America's Team." *Dallas Morning News* writer Henry Tatum suggests that the Dallas Cowboys changed the narrative of Dallas from "the city that killed John F. Kennedy" to the home of "America's Team"—the silver and blue Dallas Cowboys. On a Monday following a Cowboy game, you did not need to ask if they won or lost—you could feel it in the air. The Cowboys were a big deal in Big D.

I met my wife, Susan Setliff, in the fall of 1973. Her family moved to Dallas from Lubbock, Texas, in 1960, and she graduated from Thomas Jefferson High School in North Dallas. Her parents had roots in West Texas but, to her regret, they lived in Portales, New Mexico, for a few months and that is where she was born. So, technically, she is not a native Texan, but she is for all practical purposes a true Texan. She grew up near the Preston Hollow area of Dallas just 10 miles south of where I grew up in Richardson. Her dad's family were members of the Church of Christ, and her great uncle was a Church of Christ minister. Her mother, Edna Bridwell, grew up in the Baptist Church and she later become a member of the Church of Christ after she married Duane Setliff. Edna brought a welcome diversity of thought from her Baptist experience. West Texans are friendly, down to earth, and resilient. So, the culture of fast-paced and less friendly Big D was an adjustment for her family. Her mother remarked that the first time she sent to the grocery store, no one said "hello." Edna said, "If I knew how to find the way out of our new neighborhood I would have driven back to Lubbock." Edna and Duane bought an older home in an established neighborhood near Midway and Northwest Highway. It was a wonderful neighborhood with a real sense of community and a great place for Susan and her sister, Gail, to grow up.

I started to work for the Dallas-based Alford, Meroney CPA firm in Dallas in 1972. My first audit job was at Southwest Airmotive Corporation, located at Love Field. Susan was working there at the same time, but we never met. Susan attended Oklahoma Christian College for a year and a half, studying business administration. Her mother said that she served her time there "like a prison sentence." Susan did not want to attend college, but her mother insisted that she go for at least two years, and she fulfilled that commitment by attending her last semester at Stephen F. Austin University in Nacogdoches, Texas. Despite her reluctance, she learned some valuable skills in those two years, and she landed a secretarial job at Southwest Airmotive. The environment in 1972 at that company would be considered toxic today for a female employee and subject to litigation. The men there were crude and disrespectful of women. While she was working there, her grandfather passed away; the funeral was going to be held in West Texas so she asked her boss if she could have a couple of days off to attend the funeral. Her boss said no to the time off—so she quit on the spot! As they were headed to west Texas for the funeral Susan told her mother that she had quit her job. Edna was shocked: "What are you going to do?" Susan confidently responded. "I'll just get a better job."

She learned later that her boss told a coworker, "She'll come back." Uh, no! She did not!

R. L. Thorton was mayor of Dallas in the 1950s. His motto for the city was "Keep the Dirt Flying." Dallas was a real estate driven town and home to the Trammell Crow Company, the largest real estate development company in the USA. Another spinoff of the Trammell Crow Company was Lincoln Property Company, headed by Mack Pogue. Susan quickly landed a new job as an administrative assistant with a top commercial real estate brokerage company co-owned by Jack Pogue, who was Mack's twin brother. This was a dynamic company with several young brokers and the "who's who" of the Dallas real estate companies came through that office every day. The "dirt was flying" in Dallas, and Susan had a front seat to the action. Jack Pogue's office was in the Turtle Creek area just north of downtown and just down the street from the prestigious city of Highland Park.

Susan experienced the dynamic flow of the real estate business of Dallas while working for Jack Pogue, and she often had interactions with W. A. Criswell, a friend of Jack's. Criswell was the senior pastor of the First Baptist Church in downtown Dallas. Criswell was a highly influential character in Dallas. In 1956, Criswell gave two fiery speeches at the annual Baptist Conference on Evangelism at Columbia, South Carolina. His Texas-style message shocked the attendees in South Carolina. He was for racial and religious segregation and suggested strongly that Black people did not possess the same kind of soul before God that white people had. Kristin Kobes Du Mez says this regarding Criswell in her book, *Jesus and John Wayne—How White Evangelicals Corrupted a Faith and Fractured a Nation*:

> *"To White Americans who were willing to listen, the civil rights movement argued that America had been a country of liberty and justice for all. Evangelicals' response to civil rights varied particularly in the early stages of the movement. It is easily forgotten, but some evangelicals—especially those who would come to constitute the 'evangelical Left'—were supporters of civil rights. Others, primarily*

> *fundamentalists and southerners, were staunch opponents. In the*
> *aftermath of the Civil War, the Lost Cause of the Confederate South*
> *had blended with Christian theology to produce a distinctly south-*
> *ern variation of civil religion, one that upheld Robert E. Lee as*
> *a patron saint. In this tradition, W. A. Criswell of First Baptist*
> *Dallas (Robert Jeffress' future home) crusaded against integration*
> *as 'a denial of all that we believe in.' To such opponents, civil rights*
> *activism was a sign of disruption and disorder; many denounced*
> *Martin Luther King Jr. as a communist agitator.*"[33]

Welcome to Dallas in the 1950s. Criswell had modified his views on segregation somewhat by the time Susan encountered him, but he, along with other
influential white clergy, worked against desegregation that had become the
law of the land.

I worked for a mid-sized, Dallas-based CPA firm for the first six years
after I graduated from college. The firm had several oil and gas clients, and it
was my hope that I would eventually be hired by one of those clients to escape
the long hours and treadmill of public accounting. The oil and gas industry
seemed exciting and an appropriate Texan thing to pursue, like Jett Rink in
the movie *Giant*. I had some family experience with oil wells. My grandfather,
Walter Mackoy, farmed around Frisco and Grayson County, and in the 1930s
he bought a 75-acre farm about three miles outside of Whitesboro. Walter had
a hunch that there might be oil under the sandy loam soil on that flat, desolate
patch of land in Grayson County. Life on that little farm was hard during the
Depression for Walter and Cleo Mackoy, and it could be said that they were
dirt poor. In the late 1940s, several wells had been drilled south of Whitesboro,
but all were abandoned as dry holes. In the spring of 1952, the Kerr-McGee
No. 1 well was drilled approximately 2 ½ miles west of the Mackoy farm. It,
too, was a dry hole. The nearest producing oil well to the Mackoy farm was
located some six miles to the north. My mother and dad, along with their two-
year-old son (me), were spending the night on the Mackoy farm the day after
Thanksgiving in 1952. That night the Seitz & Seitz oil company was drilling
a well on the south side of that 75-acre farm. Around midnight my parents

and grandparents heard a ruckus coming from the drilling operation. Seitz and Seitz had punched the pipe past 4,500 feet. Walter got out of bed and hastily walked down to the drill site to see what was going on. He stood next to a worker and watched the commotion around the well. The worker said to Walter, "I don't know who owns this farm, but he's a rich man." The Mackoy No. 1 well had hit—it was a free-flowing "gusher" producing approximately 1,000 barrels a day. They drilled two more wells on that site, and they also successfully produced. Walter and Cleo were able to buy a small house in Whitesboro, and my grandmother drove a new car every three years that was purchased at the "Ford House" in Whitesboro. They were able to live a middle-class lifestyle and helped fund the building of a little church on the east side of town. This is a classic Texas story, a real-life version of Jett Rink hitting oil on a little sliver of land on the fictional Reata Ranch. So, to me, the oil "bidness" seemed like it would be exciting. However, that was not meant to be. I was never assigned to any of the oil and gas clients. Instead, I was assigned to the annual audit of a North Dallas real estate company, Folsom Investments, Inc.

Robert "Bob" Folsom was a Dallas native who started his own real estate company that built apartments, residential lot developments, golf courses, suburban office buildings, and grocery-anchored retail centers. He was a four-sport athlete in college and played for both Army and SMU. He played alongside Doak Walker who won the Heisman trophy while at SMU. Folsom started the Dallas Chapparals, an ABA basketball team that later became the San Antonio Spurs. He was mayor of Dallas from 1976 to 1981. In the spring of 1978, the chief financial officer of Folsom Investments, Ray Gressett, offered me the job of vice president of finance. I nearly jumped out of my chair when he made the offer—it was a "dream job." They had their own small office building in Addison, Texas, with a cool outdoor atrium in the middle boasting a waterfall and stream. They were one of the few companies at the time with an "office casual" dress code—no coat and ties required!

Bob Folsom did not come across as a man of the people. He was an authoritarian leader who sequestered himself in his office, guarded by his administrative assistant who had the personality of a drill sergeant with a migraine. He did understand real estate. In a Monday morning staff meeting he passed along a pearl of wisdom that in my experience has proven to be wise. A young developer in the retail division was pitching a site for a shopping center to be located in Rockwall, and he ended his presentation with this commonly known refrain: "Mr. Folsom, this opportunity has the three most important things needed for success—location, location, location!" Folsom stood up and forcefully told the group with a full Texas accent: "Boys, it is not about location, location, location. It's always about timing, timing, timing." That proved to be good advice.

At the end of the 1970s federal court orders dismantled the city's old at-large election system that had allowed Dallas to run by a white oligarchy who prevented any district representation of the black community. So, Bob Folsom became mayor when it was now possible for an independent city council member to be elected to office. Elsie Faye Heggins was a Black community organizer who had been involved in investigating the mistreatment of Black homeowners in Fair Park and conflicts with the city council over administration of the "War on Poverty" programs. When Heggins was elected to the Dallas City Council in 1980, she was seen on the local evening TV news every Wednesday night after the weekly council meeting. She would humbly challenge Mayor Folsom on issues, and she directly told the white members of the council that they were racists. In his book, "The Accommodation" Jim Shutze describes how these interactions between Higgins and Folsom went:

> *"When Mrs. Heggins was giving him the business, the body language of Mayor Folsom was worth a million words. Accustomed to Black people who spoke in answers, not questions, and never in accusations, the former SMU footballer and millionaire apartment developer took even the most timorously expressed opposition from Mrs. Higgins as if it were a savage body blow. Most but not all of the time, Folsom managed to not shout and waggle a parental finger at Mrs. Higgins. But he seemed to suffer excruciating physical pain whenever she spoke to him, twisting and writhing in his seat, holding his head and grimacing. At every Wednesday council meeting,*

Heggins and Folsom reenacted this danse macabre again for the television cameras, and every Wednesday evening on the six o'clock news it played to raves in the Black community, each of the mayor's grimaces earning Mrs. Heggins another heart-felt wave uncritical devotion from her followers"[34]

This was new territory for the Dallas City Council when Elise Faye Heggins stood up to call out the historical racism of Dallas to the mayor of Dallas—on television. She demonstrated unusual courage and resilience. The white political leaders of Dallas were not used to being challenged by anyone outside of their narrow clique.

My last interaction with Bob Folsom was not a good one. In the spring of 1980, my boss at Folsom Investments was going through some mid-life issues and decided to resign his position as CFO. At 29 years of age, I saw this as an opportunity for me to become the CFO. The company had just finished a new mid-rise office building in the Bent Tree area of North Dallas, and I was preparing to move there into my new office. In June 1980, Bob Folsom called me in and said that he had decided to bring a previous accounting person who had worked there back to the company. He told me that I had an excellent work ethic, had done good work, but that I made too much money and that my new office was too big—so I was fired with two months' severance pay. When I heard that, *my* body language gave away my disdain.

In a few weeks after the mayor fired me, I landed a job as a regional controller for the new high-rise office building division of Lincoln Property Company located in the Turtle Creek area of North Dallas. Lincoln was the second largest real estate company in the city. Its CEO was Mack Pogue. Susan knew a lot of the people who worked for Lincoln and had a good understanding of the real estate culture in Dallas. When I was interviewing for the LPC job, I briefly met Mack Pogue in the hallway and he said, "I'm the only old guy here, and we aren't hiring any more." He was 43 years old at the time. The high-rise office group had five key players, 27 to 32 years old, when I started there. It was a fast moving, entrepreneurial, and creative company. The real estate industry was the "dot com" of my era. Our high-rise office group was building Lincoln Centre, a mixed-use complex with 1.5 million square feet of office space, a 522-room hotel, and an upscale private athletic club. It is located at the intersection of LBJ Freeway and the Dallas North Tollway. One of the most popular TV shows in the 1980s was the prime-time soap opera *Dallas*. The premise of the show is the story of an affluent and feuding Texas family who own an independent oil company and live on a large cattle ranch. The opening credits of the show include sweeping shots of the Dallas skyline and expansive ranches and, as the letters D-A-L-L-A-S pop-up on the screen, the silver Lincoln Centre building glimmers in the background. The show presents Dallas as a wealthy and glamorous city living up to the lyrics of "Texas Our Texas." However, this was the image of *North Dallas,* ignoring South Dallas and the segregation at the core of the city's history.

In 1988, I became the executive vice president of finance and administration for Lincoln Property Company and reported directly to Mack Pogue. He had a significant western art collection made up of oil paintings and bronze sculptures displayed in the main entrance and hallway to the downtown corporate. It was an impressive collection. Stepping onto the mahogany herringbone floor in the reception area you were greeted by a large, famous original bronze sculpture cast by Frederic Remington in 1903, called *Off the Range*. The sculpture depicts four cowboys riding galloping horses while shooting pistols and shouting. Remington said that the sculpture suggested the bravado and energy that characterized the frontier way of life.

The corporate offices of LPC projected a rugged, wealthy cowboy culture—and you had better buckle up when you entered the conference room to negotiate a deal. I would routinely go in and of Mack Pogue's office multiple times a day. As I walked through his office door, on my right was a bronze statue on a pedestal. It was a statue of the mythical American movie cowboy, John Wayne, portrayed in his classic swagger stance. It always struck me as odd. Maybe you were supposed to genuflect before the idol of American male masculinity before entering the "holy of holies"—the office of the Chief Executive Officer. Kristin Dobes Du Mez in her book, *Jesus and John Wayne—How*

White Evangelicals Corrupted a Faith and Fractured a Nation says this about the hero worship surrounding John Wayne:

> *"The products Christians consume shape the faith they inhabit. Today, what it means to be a "conservative evangelical" is as much about culture as it is about theology. This is readily apparent in the heroes they celebrate...As the onscreen embodiment of the heroic cowboy and idealized American soldier, and also and outspoken activist in real life, John Wayne became an icon of rugged American manhood for generations of conservatives".*[35]

The Dallas culture idealized male swagger and bravado and had no need to understand its history. In 1997, Dallas Mayor Ron Kirk said: *"To many people around the world, Dallas is defined by three things: the Kennedy assassination, the Dallas Cowboys, and an international popular television show."* These are descriptions that do not predate 1960 and do not address the true fabric of the city.

In early 1988, I was asked to step out of my regional finance VP job at Lincoln Property Company and be put on a five-person "SWAT team" at Lincoln. The purpose of the SWAT team was to spend several weeks analyzing the financial viability of Lincoln—and determine if we were broke. The Savings and Loan Crisis was in full swing. Lax regulatory oversight of the S&Ls, along with unsound real estate lending, caused real estate values to collapse. The SWAT team reported back that while we had more than $50 million of cash, we had more than $4 billion in debt that was under water due to the value of the real estate. Half of that debt was personally guaranteed by approximately 60 individual partners in the firm. Later that year, the First Republic Bank of Dallas failed, and the following year MCorp (Mercantile National Bank of Dallas) failed along with many S&Ls and other banks. Many S&L and bank executives were convicted of fraud and served jail time. There were large layoffs in the real estate industry. It took approximately five years for Lincoln Property Company to restructure its debt and become solvent again. People had to sell their cars, homes, and significantly cut back their affluent lifestyles. First

Republic Bank was taken over by outsiders—a bank from Charlotte, North Carolina! Dallas had lost its swagger. John Wayne had fallen flat on his face.

The Dallas story and history is really one of two cities—ironically, North and South. Dallas is historically one of the most spatially segregated cities in the United States. From the early days of history, African Americans lived south of the Trinity River in "South Dallas" and Hispanics lived in West Dallas. The poor and marginalized were in peripheral areas that were food and business deserts. If you grew up in North Dallas County, you did not go to South Dallas unless you went to the City Zoo. It was out of sight, out of mind. Many African Americans lost the small homes (that they had paid for) because of use of eminent domain for what the city called "slum clearance." This was done in areas such as the Trinity River basin and to black-owned houses in Fair Park. Black-owned homes in Oak Cliff in the 1940s and 1950s were subjected to random bombings that caused owners to have to relocate, often incurring a financial loss. The following are some of the hardships and disadvantages that minorities faced in Dallas history:

- 1902: Texas Poll Tax law stripped black citizens of the right to vote, and African Americans were excluded from voting in Democratic Party primary elections

- 1907: Dallas charter revised to allow racial segregation in public schools, housing, amusements, and churches

- 1916: Dallas charter amended to legitimate residential segregation

- 1922: Ku Klux Klan candidates carry election in Dallas County

- 1930: Dallas charter restricted African Americans access to public office by requiring all candidates to run at large and on a nonpartisan basis

I attended segregated schools in Richardson, Texas for 12 years. There were two black students who attended my high school during my senior year—but there were around 3,000 students in attendance. Segregation is a regrettable and significant part of the history of Dallas County. The history of Dallas is relatively short—a city that grew rapidly and on the north side of town always felt "new," Dallas growth ramped up after World War I and the new residents who moved in from other parts of the country did not know why the city was so separated racially between the north and south sides of the Trinity River. Until the late 1970s, the city and county were controlled by a wealthy, elite, small group of white men driven by profit and privilege.

Dallas County was also a city of churches, but segregated churches that did not address the inequities resulting from the racial divide in the community. This is a profound contradiction. Not that long ago in Texas, the institution of slavery was illegal under Mexican rule. There was a chance to be different. What if it had remained a free state? What if it had been an "emblem of freedom" and had "sent out its radiance to nations near and far" as the proud description in the state song touts?

If only these questions had been asked and made famous instead of the most notable question in Dallas history, "Who shot J.R.?" *

* *From the last episode in 1980 of the TV show Dallas*

Chapter 9

HAMILTON PARK

I never saw the popular television show *Walt Disney's Wonderful World of Color* while I was growing up in Richardson, Texas. The Abrams Road Church of Christ met at 5:30 p.m. each Sunday night—in addition to the worship assembly held on Sunday morning. The Disney show came on at 6:00 p.m. on Sundays and was usually over by the time we got home. Also, we had a black-and-white TV, so it would have only been *Walt Disney's Wonderful World* at our house. I remember people leaving quickly after the evening church service in September of 1956 to see the Ed Sullivan show because Elvis Presly was making his first appearance on that stage. Sunday nights were sometimes different with guest speakers, a performance by the touring Harding College Chorus, or maybe a short service followed by "dinner on the grounds." One Sunday night the members of the Hamilton Park Church of Christ (now the Greenville Avenue Church of Christ) just down the road came and participated in a joint worship service with our church. The Hamilton Park Church was an all-Black congregation. Abrams Road was an all-white congregation. Church was segregated at that time when I was probably around 11 years of age. I remember standing next to my grandfather, Clint Wallis, on the church front lawn after the service where everyone was talking, and he introduced me to a Black man who was a leader in that congregation. Everyone was very pleasant and smiling. It was the first time I had ever shaken hands with a Black person. I just had never had the opportunity. A couple of Sunday nights later, the Abrams Road Church members went to the Hamilton Park Church building to participate in their Sunday night worship service. I still remember the powerful singing of that congregation. I had never heard such beautiful and powerful a capella singing like was sung that night.

The Hamilton Park Church of Christ was located on the south side of Richardson near a relatively new Black middle-class subdivision know as Hamilton Park. The neighborhood had a park, a K-12 grade school (Richardson Independent School District), a shopping center, and an apartment complex. Although I lived in close proximity to Hamilton Park, I never heard why this segregated black neighborhood existed or the story of its origin.

Hamilton Park was established in 1954 because of several black homes being bombed in South Dallas in 1950. In 1953, a Dallas bond election provided for the demolition of Black-owned housing near Love Field to be demolished so that the airport could be expanded. There was a drastic shortage of housing for Blacks in Dallas and the white community was unwilling to support integrated neighborhoods. The conspirators who bombed the homes in South Dallas were never brought to justice by the white leaders, but they saw the establishment of Hamilton Park as an effort to address those crimes against the Black community. While Hamilton Park provided some hope for a few Black middle class families, the Dallas policy of geographical segregation still continued. There were no theaters, swimming pools, restaurants, or department stores for Black people near the homes in Hamilton Park. For those services, Hamilton Park residents' closest option was to drive into Dallas to the Thomas and Hall Area that was located near downtown.

Even though I lived just down the road from Hamilton Park I was naïve and ignorant regarding the reason and causes for the segregation of our church and our school district.

My mother worked in the payroll department of the Richardson Independent School District, and she got me and my friend Larry James jobs working on a maintenance crew for the school district during the summer. We would plant grass; hoe weeds; clean, buff, and wax miles of linoleum floors, and whatever manual labor they could come up with for us to do. One of the older men who were part of the permanent employees of the school district was Mr. Floyd. When my brother worked there after me Mr. Floyd would call him "Cuz." The crew usually consisted of half a dozen guys raking in the minimum wage of $1.25 per hour. The last summer we worked there our work crew included two young men from the Hamilton Park High School, the segregated all-Black school nearby. This was the first time I was able to spend time with young African American guys who were my age. We all got along well, worked hard, and shared a lot of laughs. However, one afternoon there was an incident at the 7-Eleven located near the intersection of Belt Line Road and Coit Road in Richardson, Texas, that is burned into my brain—something I will never forget. Larry James recalls this incident in his excellent book, *The Wealth of the Poor* as follows:

> *In a summer groundskeeping job with the Richardson Schools, I worked with two boys my age named Carl and Leotis, who lived in Hamilton Park, the African American part of the school district before Richardson desegregated the schools according to court order in Brown v. Board of Education. Amazingly, but typical for the time and place, I had never been friends or worked with an African American.*
>
> *We did what boys do and compared notes on each other's lives. They were like me but without all of the privileges and systemic advantages that came with being born white. The three of us came from the same kind of families in terms of economic class. Our fathers were hard working men with limited educations who made good lives for themselves and their families. We had a lot in common than whatever dynamics made us different—except for skin color and what that meant in 1968.*
>
> *This ugly reality became clear to me one hot July afternoon when we took a break from working at the high school football field and*

walked over to the corner 7-Eleven to get a cold drink. We were hors-ing around and not making much trouble, but the manager abruptly asked my two friends to leave. He gave no reason for his action. To me he asked, "May I help you son?" I told him I didn't need anything, and I followed my friends out the door. I still remember the terrible silence that pressed on us the rest of the day.

I asked what had had happened.

My friends didn't really try to explain to me, but it was clear that they we were invited to leave only because of the color of their skin. This all sounds so terribly naïve and ridiculous today but for me it was near, new, surprising awakening. My first friendship with two young African Americans was extremely positive and, thus, this new awakening to the reality the hidden racism in the city of Dallas was very confusing to me.

These young men were just like me, except they couldn't go into all the places I could enter during that summer. They were just like me, but I'd been schooled by my environment and the people I trusted to believe that black people were not like me at all. This was undoubt-edly the most crippling lie of my childhood....

Sadly, the church as I knew it did nothing to prepare me for the real-ity of the world when it came to social issues and so many things that mattered so much at that time and continue to matter today. In my church no one ever said a word about this overarching reality of the day. Church functioned as a place of escape for a cult of people who failed to make the connection between things of the spirit and matters of the street. I know this was not the experience of all church-going people at the time, but it was mine.

I now realize that I came to resent this fact about my heritage and felt somehow cheated by the lack of relevance offered by those entrusted to provide moral guidance at such a troubled and troubling time. It is clear to me now that underneath the apparent irrelevance lurked a *virtual right-wing extremism that many had baptized and brought into the worldview of the church without giving equal time to other perspectives...*"[36]

I remember Larry standing up to the 7-Eleven manager and saying, "My friends are just like me; if you can't serve them, you're not going to serve me." Then we all walked out.

At first I didn't realize what was going down. It never crossed my mind that there would be any reason for a confrontation. We were just trying to get out of the 100-degree Texas heat and buy a Coke on our afternoon break. We all were well-behaved young men who were generally soft-spoken and worked hard. I had not witnessed this kind of hate firsthand. Why? Because I had been living in an isolated "white bubble," insulated from the real world.

The Richardson Independent School District was not integrated until 1969 when the Hamilton Park K-12 school was closed. The Hamilton Park school was reopened in 1975 as a magnet school that was integrated.

We went to church on Sunday morning, Sunday night, and Wednesday night and believed that our church was "restoring" the way God wanted the church to be. But as Larry said, our churches offered a "lack of relevance" to what was going on in the world. We were taught strict morality codes that emphasized separation from the world. (i.e., I was not allowed to go to dances in high school). In Isaiah 58:1-12 NIV, the prophet talks about how Israel boasts about how "We have fasted."

True Fasting

[58] "Shout it aloud, do not hold back.
 Raise your voice like a trumpet.
Declare to my people their rebellion
 and to the descendants of Jacob their sins.
2 For day after day they seek me out;
 they seem eager to know my ways,
as if they were a nation that does what is right
 and has not forsaken the commands of its God.

They ask me for just decisions
 and seem eager for God to come near them.
3 'Why have we fasted,' they say,
 'and you have not seen it?
Why have we humbled ourselves,
 and you have not noticed?'
"Yet on the day of your fasting, you do as you please
 and exploit all your workers.
4 Your fasting ends in quarreling and strife,
 and in striking each other with wicked fists.
You cannot fast as you do today
 and expect your voice to be heard on high.
5 Is this the kind of fast I have chosen,
 only a day for people to humble themselves?
Is it only for bowing one's head like a reed
 and for lying in sackcloth and ashes?
Is that what you call a fast,
 a day acceptable to the Lord?
6 "Is not this the kind of fasting I have chosen:
to loose the chains of injustice
 and untie the cords of the yoke,
to set the oppressed free
 and break every yoke?
7 Is it not to share your food with the hungry
 and to provide the poor wanderer with shelter—
when you see the naked, to clothe them,
 and not to turn away from your own flesh and blood?
8 Then your light will break forth like the dawn,
 and your healing will quickly appear;
then your righteousness will go before you,
 and the glory of the Lord will be your rear guard.

9 Then you will call, and the Lord will answer;
 you will cry for help, and he will say: Here am I.
"If you do away with the yoke of oppression,
 with the pointing finger and malicious talk,
¹⁰ and if you spend yourselves in behalf of the hungry
 and satisfy the needs of the oppressed,
then your light will rise in the darkness,
 and your night will become like the noonday.
¹¹ The Lord will guide you always;
 he will satisfy your needs in a sun-scorched land
 and will strengthen your frame.
You will be like a well-watered garden,
 like a spring whose waters never fail.
¹² Your people will rebuild the ancient ruins
 and will raise up the age-old foundations;
you will be called Repairer of Broken Walls,
 Restorer of Streets with Dwellings.

Our churches were primarily focused on getting the rituals right and adhering to "strict moral codes" and isolating ourselves from the world. Is this the kind of fast that God has chosen? Verse six hits home with me:

> ⁶ Is not this the kind of fasting I have chosen: to loosen the chains of injustice and untie the cords of the yoke, to set the oppressed free and break every yoke?

Was our church doing a "right fast"? How could it ignore the oppression brought on by the sin of the belief in white supremacy?

We were watching "Our Wonderful World" on a black-and-white TV— and missed out on seeing "God's Wonderful World of Color."

Chapter 10

STATEMENT OF ATTITUDE

I was not well-traveled in the days of my youth, so venturing anywhere outside of Dallas County was exciting. My grandmother, Winnie Wallis, had one sister, Alice Davis, who lived in Kensett, Arkansas. On a few occasions our family would load up in the family Chevrolet along with my dad's two sisters and my grandparents and drive to Arkansas to visit relatives. Visiting the "Natural State" was exciting. From the backseat window, I'd watch the flat landscape of North Texas disappear and the tall trees, rolling green hills, and natural flowing rivers appear. Aunt Alice and Uncle Kenneth lived on a farm outside of town and it had a pond for fishing, a tree house, and plenty of first and second cousins to hang out with. In addition, a lot of skinny trees surrounded the pond. Uncle Kenneth, Sr., wanted them cleared out, so he gave the cousins axes and let us start chopping. As a young boy it was a thrill to swing an axe at a tree and yell, "Timber!"

In addition, my dad's first cousin, Dr. Kenneth Davis, Jr., was a music professor at nearby Harding College located in Searcy, Arkansas. He directed the Harding College Acapella Chorus which toured all over the U.S. and internationally. We would usually be there during our visits, and we would walk around the Harding campus. I remember going into the "new" American Heritage Center building and being so impressed with the color console television in the lobby. The Harding campus was relatively small at the time, but the red-brick buildings surrounding a large tree-filled lawn looked like a college campus straight out of a movie. Kenneth had access to the campus, and since classes were usually out when we were there, we could use some of the amenities. I remember one time the adults talking about taking all the kids over to the college swimming pool but that "mixed bathing" was against the rules there. I had no idea what "mixed bathing" was, but my first impulse was that I was against it. Turns out the Arkansas and Tennessee cousins knew what this was—it meant boys and girls could not go swimming together at the same time because of modesty issues related to swimwear. We did not get to go swimming.

During my senior year of high school, I was thinking about colleges. My plan was to become a lawyer and attend a "Church of Christ" college. My two choices were essentially Abilene Christian College or Harding College. Abilene was the more prestigious of the two and had around 3,000 students compared to 2,000 at Harding. I went with a group from the Abrams Road church one fall weekend in 1967 to visit the Abilene campus. I heard the ACC band playing in the old field house and they sounded pretty good. I was going to try and get some kind of financial aid for being in the band. The campus was sandy with small windblown trees and the buildings were a beige brick that blended in with the West Texas landscape. I had friends from church that were going to one of these two schools. I decided to go to Harding. I think the trees and red brick were the deciding factors. Also, my older cousin Pat Malcik was already at Harding, and I had been on the campus several times. Being in a senior class of 1,000 students in high school, the smaller size of Harding had an appeal. Oh, and I got a $200 per year scholarship for being in the Harding Band. (Note: I dropped out of the band after about three weeks to play intramural flag football.)

Harding College required all undergraduate students to attend a daily chapel service Monday through Thursday in the administration building auditorium around 11:00 am. The chapel program was about 30 minutes long beginning with announcements made by the college president followed by singing hymns and one or two prayers. The remaining time would be reserved for a speaker to deliver some type of spiritual message, a musical presentation, a guest lecture on a relative topic of the day, or a short bit put on by one of the social clubs on campus. Occasionally, a Christian celebrity like Pat Boone would make an appearance. The 1972 Harding yearbook, *The Petit Jean,* described daily chapel as a "short opportunity for repose from the monotony of classes." The good news was that it was short. During my freshman year at Harding, they had two split the chapel into two gatherings due to the growth of the student body to almost 2,000 people. I was in the second chapel service on March 20, 1969, when, after the worship period, Dr. Cliff Ganus got up to the podium to address an ad hoc student committee report on racial problems existing at the school. It included a list of specific steps they hoped could be taken to improve racial relations at Harding. Most of the Black students had already attended the first chapel and heard Ganus give a defensive speech in response to the criticisms the student committee had brought to him. About 20 Black students along with a few white supporters attended the second chapel service and sat in the unassigned seats in the front row and then as a protest walked out of the speech by Ganus while raising their hands in a Black Power salute. I remember sitting there with my mouth open wondering what was happening. I was a clueless 18-year-old freshman who did nothing. Now, I wish I had walked out too—but I was not prepared to understand the moment. The event was significant enough to be covered by the Little Rock press.

Harding College was founded in 1924 and was a segregated school until 1963 when three African American students—Lewis Brown, Walter Cunningham, and David Johnson—were admitted. Elijah Anthony and Howard Wright were the first African American undergraduate students to earn bachelor's degrees from Harding in 1968. After World War II, many Church of Christ college students began to view desegregation as a moral choice that could be backed up by Scripture. Black members of the Churches of Christ had the limited choice of attending Pepperdine College in Los Angeles or the new Southwestern Christian College in Terrell, Texas. Seeking to study the teachings of the Restoration Movement, Norman Adamson applied for admission to Harding in 1953 and was at first accepted but his application was rejected once the college administrators found out that he was Black. In 1954, with the ruling of the Supreme Court against segregation, many of the students at Harding began to express opinions in *The Bison*, the school newspaper, that Harding should take the lead and desegregate the school. In the fall of 1957, several Harding students approached the student body president, Bill Floyd, about demanding change from Harding's President George Benson. But Benson was a right-wing, outspoken leader who believed segregation was intended by God—what some call "theological racism." However, Bill Floyd agreed to circulate a "Statement of Attitude" for signature by students and faculty to then be submitted to the Board of Trustees and Benson. The document read as follows:

> *To the Administration and Board of Trustees of Harding College*
>
> *A number of members of the Harding community are deeply concerned about the problem of racial discrimination. Believing that it is wrong for Christians to make among people distinctions which God has not made, they sincerely desire that Harding College make clear to the world that she firmly believes in the principles of the fatherhood of God and the brotherhood of man. To that end, the undersigned individuals wish to state that they are ready to accept as members of the Harding community all academically and morally qualified applicants, without regard to arbitrary distinctions such as color or social level; that they will treat such individuals with the consideration and dignity appropriate to human beings created in the image of God; and that they will at all times face quietly, calmly, patiently, and sympathetically and social pressures intensified by this action.*
>
> *Furthermore, the undersigned individuals wish it clearly understood that this statement of attitude is by no means intended as an attempt to precipitate action by the Administration or Board of Trustees of Harding College but that it is instead intended entirely as an expression of the internal readiness of the Harding community to*

end discrimination, such expression being tendered as one factor for
the consideration of the Administration and the Board of Trustees
when a reevaluation of the admission policies of Harding College
is undertaken.

More than 85% of the student body and more than 100 faculty members signed this document—a total of 946 people.[37] I am proud to say that my dad's first cousin, (and 2nd great grandson of John B. Floyd) Kenneth Davis, Jr., signed this document along with Billy Ray Cox, who was vice president of the business school when I attended Harding and one of my key business career mentors.

In Spring 2021, Hannah Wood, Harding University assistant professor and Archives and Special Collections librarian, had this to say about the event:

"Women and men of multiple generations envisioned a Harding
College where the color of a student's skin did not preclude them from
actively participating in the Harding community. They signed their
names to speak with one voice in support of this dream. They had a
voice. You have a voice."[38]

George Benson made a chapel appearance and told the students that presentation of the "Statement" was improper and the signatures were not an accurate expression of student feelings, just like the current "it was rigged" argument used by politicians today. The Board of Trustees stood by and did nothing. What a significant missed opportunity for the Harding community to stand up for the equality of all men and women.

President George Benson was an autocratic leader who had little if no regard for input from students or from a majority of the faculty. Benson's successor, Clifton Ganus, Jr., said this about Benson: "Benson called the shots, not the students. And even though there were many students that might want to be integrated, and even though there were some of us faculty members that were all for it, until he was ready for it, it didn't happen...as I said, he ran a pretty tight ship and called all the shots."[39]

J. Nelson Armstrong was the first president of Harding when it was founded in 1924. He was a student of James Harding and David Lipscomb, who were more grace-oriented than the "strict" students of Alexander Campbell. Armstrong was a pacifist who closed the doors of Cordell College and moved it to another state rather than violate his convictions regarding not serving in the armed services. He was a kind man who was open to hearing the opinions and beliefs of others even though he personally disagreed with them. He was relentlessly criticized by other Church of Christ preachers regarding his not firing a professor at Harding because of that person's belief in some form of premillennialism. He was not a Christian Nationalist. The following is from the book *For Freedom: The Biography of John Nelson Armstrong* by L. C. Sears.

> *"He was opposed to involving the college in political actions. He was willing for faculty members to follow any political course they chose, but he objected to aligning the college institutionally with political groups. In a letter of 1943 he said: "We should not do wrong to get money...Certainly we all approved of Clinton's (Davidson's) original plan to interest men in Harding College. But did this mean to turn the campaign into a defense of the U. S. Government, to regulate its tax system, even to support a political group? Who dreamed it would lead to this...Money is not worth this much as I see it...I repeat, Harding College was not established to save some form of government or to reform it."*

Armstrong believed in the equality of all races and L.C. sears said this about Armstrong:

> *"He had the same feeling for the colored races. He contributed frequently to a Negro college in Mississippi and spoke to the students at Shorter College in Little Rock, encouraging them to educate themselves and prepare for lives of constructive service."*[40]

Armstrong said this regarding being a Southerner and the "slave question":

> *"I was born and raised in Tennessee, and of Southern parents. Father was a Democrat, one that 'scratcheth not the ticket.' And if I had any*

prejudice regarding the slave question, it would be wholly Southern. But God has taught me that a Christian cannot be a partisan; that he must know that God's child must be like his Father, no respecter of persons. So I have interest, much interest, in the advancement of every race of men upon the earth; especially does my heart go out for the needy in our own country."

Armstrong was and advocate of free speech for Christians and advocated being kind and respectful of the positions of others. Armstrong said this:

"There is great need to stress the importance of maintaining freedom of speech in the kingdom of God. Intolerance is dangerous to the future and growth of the church. Most of us have an aversion to anything except what we ourselves believe and teach and as a consequence, we are intolerant of the teaching of anything that antagonizes our doctrine. All progress of truth—all truth—has always depended on free speech and progressive teachers who are not afraid to teach their honest convictions, even thought it cost life...It takes no courage to teach the things one's audience already believes.

...I am well aware of the fact that free speech has its dangers and that progressive and fearless teachers have given the world untold trouble. But are we ready to surrender free speech and to deny ourselves teachers who are not afraid? Even our deliverance from such a responsibility must come through free speech and courageous teachers. If our great-great-grandchildren enjoy the truth that we hold dear, it will be due to free speech and courageous teachers."[41]

I believe that the 946 people who signed the "Statement of Attitude" were influenced by the legacy and spirit of J. N. Armstrong. In a speech given at a Harding Alumni dinner in May of 2013, Cliff Ganus, Jr. said President Armstrong's legacy was the spirit of Harding, and I believe the "Statement of Attitude" was because of the spirit set forth by the leadership of Armstrong. However, George Benson had set the primary course of Harding on the path of patriarchal authority and Christian nationalism, which were based on the importance of having a white identity. Benson placed all of this under the umbrella of the "threat of communism."

Benson's American nationalism program was conducted through the "National Education Program" (NEP) which was incorporated as an entity separated from the college in 1954. This separation was done because the existence of the NEP within the college was preventing Harding from receiving academic accreditation. Benson appeared before the U.S. House Ways and Means Committee on May 15, 1941, to testify against a proposed tax bill that would be used to build up the U. S. military. Benson wanted to eliminate most New Deal programs and use those funds for the military. This speech got nationwide attention and opened doors to major corporations like General Motors, DuPont Chemical, Quaker Oats, Boeing Aircraft, and Gulf Oil, who made major donations to Harding. This provided funds for building nine new buildings on campus, including the administration building, library, and two auditoriums. In 1962, Ronald Regan narrated an NEP film, *The Truth about Communism*. Benson was member of the "Moral Majority" before there was one. In August of 1980, Benson spoke at a pro-Republican Moral Majority rally along with Jerry Falwell, Pat Robertson, and Ronald Reagan. George Benson was the antithesis of J. N. Armstrong, the first president of Harding College. Again, here are J. N. Armstrong's words:

> *"Money is not worth this much as I see it...I repeat, Harding College was not established to save some form of government or to reform it."*

In March 1968, one year before the walkout by Black students during Dr. Cliff Ganus's speech in the Harding chapel, two black seniors, Elijah Anthony and Howard Wright were asked to speak in chapel about racial bigotry in Churches of Christ. They spoke about how that Churches of Christ had not addressed the racial discrimination that existed in the country. Anthony told the audience that churches have "been avoiding the issue of race; we just slid over, under and around it." During his comments Wright said, "We're worried about what the world will think...How long are we going to say, 'don't buck society?' How long?" [42]

During the fall of my freshman year (1968) at Harding College I joined a men's social club, "Frater Sodalis." Harding did not have fraternities, so instead social clubs were an integral part of campus life. That year a new social club was formed by Black students on campus and its name was "Groove Phi Groove." The club was formed because those students were experiencing discrimination and not being treated as equals. I remember going to an intramural flag football game between Groove Phi Groove and Sub T-16 and the field was surrounded by hundreds of students and the tension in the air was thick. They were the two best teams, and it was a close game. I do not remember who won, but I recall it demonstrated that race relations at Harding were not what they should be. In his book, *Race and Restoration: Churches of Christ and the Black Freedom Struggle*, Barclay Key describes how unwelcome Black students felt at Harding:

> *"They faced restrictions from other clubs in their intramural participation, for example, but hostilities were much more rampant than conflicts among competing organizations. They were incensed that derogatory terms such as "boy," "Nigra," and "colored" were still used frequently when whites spoke of or to them. Entities within the college, especially a conservative think tank known as the National Education Program, consistently derided the civil rights movement by claiming that communists influenced civil rights activists. During the previous fall, Harding professor James Bales published a controversial book, "The Martin Luther King Story, with a "A Study in Apostasy, Agitation, and Anarchy" emblazoned across the top of the front cover. One black student had some of his personal property burned, and one of the most popular tunes that the pep band played at athletic events was 'Dixie.' In addition to a long list of grievances, various disciplinary measures taken by the administration against black students were perceived as unfair. Given these circumstances, it is easy to understand why black students questioned Harding's commitment to racial equality a few years after the first black students appeared on campus."[43]*

Sometime during the spring semester of 1969, Groove Phi Groove ended as a social club on campus. I searched my 1969 *Petit Jean* yearbook to see what it said about Groove Phi Groove in both the social club and student life sections. I found absolutely nothing about the chapel demonstration, and the Groove Phi Groove club was not mentioned. The name of the *Petit Jean* yearbook that year was "The Face of Harding 1969." Well, I guess it was only "The White Face of Harding."

Cliff Ganus's chapel speech in March 1969 was defensive in nature and at best tone deaf. He said he "had been prejudiced all right—prejudiced toward helping people regardless of color." He talked about how he had recently participated in a Church of Christ 1968 Race Relations Conference in Atlanta—which was a good thing, but he also described how he let the "colored maid" eat at the dinner table with his family as indication of how he was not prejudiced against Blacks. Cliff Ganus was a good man, but he was surrounded by George Benson and his cronies who were not a good influence, and I suspect they did not support his intent to avoid prejudice. Over the years, Ganus as chancellor actively recruited Black students to attend Harding. However, he, along with many others, was not prepared to understand the critical and important issues the ad hoc student committee had raised in Spring 1969. The spirit of J. N. Armstrong was severely repressed and often forgotten by the leadership of the school.

On October 31, 2021, the Harding University Administration Building built in 1952 was named in honor of Elijah Anthony and Howard Wright, the first African American students to earn bachelor's degrees from Harding. The interim president, David Burks, offered the following apology at the renaming ceremony:

> *"Racism and prejudice existed within the Harding community, and we acknowledge the pain that you felt. For this we are truly sorry. We also express tremendous gratitude for these individuals and the many students who have followed in their footsteps. Their faith,*

*courage and commitment are an inspiration to us and will continue
to be for generations of Harding students to come."*

Recall that in March 1968, Howard Wright asked: "How long are we going
to say, 'don't' buck society'? How long?"

It took 53 years.

I received an excellent liberal arts education from Harding College and
obtained a valuable bachelor's degree in accounting. The business department,
led by Billy Ray Cox, was one of the best in the nation in the early 1970s. I sat
at the feet of sincere and humble Bible professors who taught me the basics of
how to study the Bible and the importance of being part of a Christian community. I have many wonderful friends and acquaintances from the Harding
community. I have been a supporter of Harding over the years, including
serving for four years as chairman of the President's Council and was a member of the Board of Trustees from 2004 to 2013. In my opinion, Harding
leadership has operated with "Exceptionalism" as a core belief and guiding
principle. This is a belief that the Harding University community is especially
morally unique and superior to other colleges and universities. This attitude
of superiority would also apply in relation to other Church of Christ schools.
This "Exceptionalism" is based on poor historical knowledge and carefully
crafted antidotal comparisons that exaggerate accomplishment and diminish
or erase failures. For example—Groove Phi Groove does not exist in the 1969
Petit Jean. This history was ignored by the blinding belief in Exceptionalism.
American Exceptionalism's blinding light still attempts to eradicate the study
of both the good and bad of our history as a nation.

Built in 1950, Armstrong Hall is the oldest men's dormitory and is one
of the least visible and most unattractive buildings at Harding. It's been almost
70 years since the "Statement of Attitude" was rejected by George Benson, yet
his name is on the largest and most prominent building on campus.

On June 2, 2020, just one week after the death of George Floyd, Harding
alumnus Jackson House circulated a petition in favor of changing the name
of the "George S. Benson Auditorium." The petition advocated changing of

the name to honor fellow Black alumnus Botham S. Jean who was murdered in his apartment by an off-duty Dallas police officer in 2018. The 26-year-old Jean was a popular person on the Harding campus when as a student he often led singing at the daily chapel service. He received a degree in accounting and management information and worked for Price Waterhouse Cooper. The petition had significant traffic on social media and more than 10,000 signatures within 24 hours. Jackson House explained Benson's resistance to desegregation and quoted his 1956 chapel speech, "Harding College and the Colored Problem." Harding University's president at the time said "Harding University condemns racism in its many forms and is working to better understand how to do so." The House petition had reached 18,000 signatures when Harding President Bruce McClarty announced the name of the auditorium would not be changed. Instead, he announced the formation of a task force made up of Board members, employees, alumni, and students tasked with determining things to be done on campus to honor African American history, presence, and the accomplishments of Black students on the Harding campus.[44] This led to the renaming the Administration Building after Elijah Anthony and Howard Wright and the placing of a memorial to Botham Jean on the main part of the campus.[45]

> *"Therefore, confess your sins to each other and pray for each other so that you may be healed.... James 5:16 NIV*

Chapter 11

CUFFLINKS

When I went to work for United Dominion Realty Trust in early 2001, I made many trips to the company's original corporate headquarters in Richmond, Virginia. I heard the people in Richmond often refer to the Civil War as "The War of Northern Aggression." While growing up in Dallas, I had not heard that phrase used but I understood it spoke directly to the Southern perspective of the Civil War. I was taught as a child the Civil War was not about slavery, rather it was about states' rights and a battle between the Southern way of life and the ungodly industrial North. After the loss of the Civil War there was conscious effort to rewrite history and justify the defeat and great loss of life. A revised narrative of the war evolved referred to as the myth of the "Lost Cause." I grew up hearing the story of the "Lost Cause" as historical fact... almost as a religious narrative of what happened. It invoked a romanticized nostalgic view of the past to which many white people wished to return. The following are some of the claims of the "Lost Cause":

- States' rights were the cause of the Civil War, not the institution of slavery.

- No need to abolish slavery—it was a benevolent institution and possibly would go away on its own.

- Robert E. Lee was the greatest general in American history.

- Ulysses S. Grant was an incompetent butcher and only won the war by overwhelming force.

- Confederate General James Longstreet was responsible for the loss of Gettysburg

- The Confederacy was a noble endeavor to preserve the "Southern way of life" from attacks by northerners and Black people.

If the United States was a "Christian Nation," how could we let a civil war cause the deaths of more than 600,000 people? Both the North and South each believed God was on their side. It came to be viewed that God would be revealed to be on the side that won the war.

The perspective of the War in the South balanced on two major points:

1. The individual state was sovereign—and even had the right to secede from the Union.

2. Slavery was an expedient part of the economy of the South but also ordained by God.

The constitution of the Confederacy, ratified on March 11, 1861, officially declared the South as a uniquely Christian nation when in the Preamble it invoked "the favor and guidance of Almighty God."

After the Confederate forces opened fire on Fort Sumter in April of 1861 most of the churches in the North supported the war on the side of the Union. The Union perspective of the War generally hinged on the following three principles:

1. America occupied a unique place in the history of the world with its democratic ideals and institutions and Christian values, standing as the special leader of civilization's march forward.

2. A millennial view: A victory by the North would prepare for the beginning of the Kingdom of God on earth.

3. An evolving view regarding slavery: God was seeking to resolve the issue of slavery more quickly and would continue to punish the North until it ended slavery.

The North initially had the goal of just preserving the Union, but eventually it began to fight a war of liberation.

Having lost the war and suffering so many casualties and losses of property, the South faced explaining why God had not given them victory. Out of this came the new narrative of the "Lost Cause" to justify what they had done.

After the Civil War, around 700 Confederate monuments were built in the United States, most of them built between the 1890s and 1950s, coinciding with the Jim Crow era of segregation. Early memorials in cemeteries were intended to be memorials mourning the death of soldiers. The United Daughters of the Confederacy, founded in the 1890s, led the movement to put hundreds of statues in city squares and parks. The purpose of these statues was to glorify people like Robert E. Lee and to defend the principles of the Confederacy. The Daughters of the Confederacy were behind the Stone Mountain carving of Robert E. Lee, Jefferson Davis, and Stonewall Jackson located near Atlanta. During this period of the Lost Cause there was a proliferation of the Confederate flag in public life. The Confederate flag was originally viewed primarily as a memorial to fallen Confederate soldiers, but it was not exclusively tied to the soldier. The Confederate (battle) flag evolved to be a celebration of the Confederacy, and many people began to express their identity as a "Southerner" with the Confederate flag. During the Civil Rights era the flag became a symbol of support for segregation and a protest against civil rights for Blacks. Eventually the Confederate flag became part of pop culture and could be found on T-shirts, hats, beach towels, jackets, etc. It became a symbol of Southern independence or being a rebellious "good ol' boy." The popular television show *The Dukes of Hazzard* that aired from 1979 to 1985 epitomizes how the Confederate flag was almost completely separated from the historical context of the Confederacy. The show featured an orange 1969 Dodge Charger driven by the "Duke boys" as they fled from local police. The car was called the "General Lee" in reference to Robert E. Lee, general of the Confederate Army. With a large Confederate battle flag painted on its roof, it boasted a horn that played the first 12 notes of the song "Dixie." Whites in America had completely desensitized their views around these symbols in relation to their origins and ties to slavery. Whites typically could not understand why the Confederate Flag was a symbol of hate to Black Americans. It should be noted that Black Americans were excluded from the decisions in America that spread Confederate flags, monuments, school names, and street names across the landscape on the United States.

When I was around 11 years old, I was given a pair of oval cufflinks to wear with my Sunday clothes. The cufflinks were black with the X shape of the blue stars of the confederate flag along with the dates of the Civil War. They were made in connection with the Centennial Anniversary of the Civil War. This was not controversial in the white world I lived in around 1962. I had been immersed in the sanitized and romanticized doctrine of the Lost Cause and cultural symbols used to promote that message.

I enrolled as a 17-year-old freshman at Harding College and was assigned to the freshman men's dorm, Armstrong Hall. The cinder block rooms were arranged in two-room suites with a bathroom connecting the rooms. I learned the other three guys who would share the suite were from Illinois. In my dad's words, I would be rooming with "Yankees." I became good friends with those young men from Illinois, but I thought I should do something to remind them I was a proud Texan and a Southerner. So, above my small study desk in the room I had two small flags crossed and mounted flat on the wall. One was the flag of the Lone Star State and the other was the Confederate Flag. No one ever really said anything about this. I did not receive a citation from the Resident Hall Director upon routine inspections of the room. It was no big deal at a time when the Harding College Band played "Dixie" at football games. Thankfully, the desk was in a corner of the room you could not see from the hallway. I did not want to include this story in this book, because I feel a sickening guilt when I think about it. However, If I want to better understand my racial identity, I must be willing to confess how I have been complicit.

Pleading ignorance is not helpful. If we do not confess, we become our own "Lost Cause."

Slavery is evil and was not ordained by God. The brutality of the "total war" eventually prosecuted by the North upon the South was also evil—and was not ordained by God. The churches of the North believed America was preparing the way for the establishment of the kingdom of God on earth and blood needed to be shed as an atonement of the sins of the nation. This sentiment of the North is exhibited in the original version of the Battle Hymn of the Republic:

Battle Hymn of the Republic
February 1862
Mine eyes have seen the coming of the Lord:
He is trampling out the vintage where the grapes of wrath
are stored.
He hath loosed the fateful lightning of His terrible swift sword:
His truth is marching on.
I have seen Him in the watch-fires of a hundred circling camps,
They have builded Him an altar in the evening dews
and damps;
I can read His righteous sentence by the dim and flaring lamps:
His day is marching on.
I have read a fiery gospel writ in burnished rows of steel
"As ye deal with my contemners, so with you my grace
shall deal;
Let the Hero, born of woman, crush the serpent with his heel,
Since God is marching on."
He has sounded forth the trumpet that shall never call retreat;
He is sifting out the hearts of men before His judgment seat:
Oh, be swift, my soul, to answer to Him! Be jubilant, my feet:
Our God is marching on.
In the Beauty of the lilies Christ was born across the sea,
With a glory in His bosom that transfigures you and me:

As He died to make men holy, let us die (teach) to make men free,
While God is marching on.

Susan and I attended Prestoncrest Church of Christ in Dallas, Texas, from 1974 to 2001, and this song was sung there on occasion during the 1990s. (The lyrics in *italics* are the lyrics we sang at church). The lyrics are propaganda for the pursuit of a religious "War of Northern Aggression"—and they say that Jesus is leading it. But this message encouraging the killing of Southern neighbors does not reconcile with the teachings of Jesus. Ronnie McBrayer says this about America's love of violence:

> *"Nowadays, as I write and speak on a wide variety of topics, this one subject—Jesus' way of non-violence—always generates the most controversy, and blisteringly so. Why is this? It is because we believe a lie, and no one likes to think his or her belief system is erroneous. But we believe that violence can somehow save us; we believe that killing will prevent future killing; be believe that warfare will produce peace. We simply trust the way of the gun more than we trust the words of and way of Jesus."*[46]

I do not believe that Jesus was leading "Sherman's March to the Sea," and it is not appropriate to glorify this pursuit by singing the "Battle Hymn of the Republic" in church—even if it's a capella.

When Robert E. Lee died in 1870 Frederick Douglass had this to say:

> *"We can scarcely take up a newspaper that is not filled with nauseating flatteries of the late Robert E. Lee...It would seem from this that the soldier who kills the most men in battle, even in a bad cause, is the greatest of Christian men, and entitled to the highest place in heaven."*[47]

Both Lee and Grant were responsible for thousands of deaths of their fellow countryman. We do not need glorified statues of them on horse placed in our city squares pretending what they did was noble. And, worshipping and idolizing flags does not justify sending people to kill and be killed in war.

The teachings of Jesus are problematic for Americans:

> [38] *"You have heard that it was said, 'Eye for eye, and tooth for tooth.'*
> *[9] But I tell you, do not resist an evil person. If anyone slaps you on*
> *the right cheek, turn to them the other cheek also. [40] And if anyone*
> *wants to sue you and take your shirt, hand over your coat as well. [41] If*
> *anyone forces you to go one mile, go with them two miles. [42] Give to*
> *the one who asks you, and do not turn away from the one who wants*
> *to borrow from you.*
>
> *[43] "You have heard that it was said, 'Love your neighbor and hate*
> *your enemy.' [44] But I tell you, love your enemies and pray for those*
> *who persecute you, [45] that you may be children of your Father in*
> *heaven. He causes his sun to rise on the evil and the good and sends*
> *rain on the righteous and the unrighteous. [46] If you love those who*
> *love you, what reward is there for that? Matthew 5:38-46 NIV*

Americans want *their country* to be their church. It's a place where it is comfortable to wear cufflinks honoring a brutal war to a church service. The following was the message on a bumper sticker that Ronnie McBrayer saw one day in traffic. It was asking a question that should be asked:

"WHO WOULD JESUS BOMB?"[48]

The real cause that was lost—was the cause that Jesus died for.

Chapter 12

LAMENT

Susan Wallis at "National Memorial for Peace and Justice

WARNING TO READERS

This chapter contains stories of terrorist attacks by white people against Black people that include descriptions of lynching and other acts of cruelty. These accounts are disturbing, shocking and may be difficult for some to process.

M y mother, Patsy Ruth Mackoy Wallis, told of one afternoon when she was very young and heard the adults in the next room talking about a lynching that had occurred somewhere in the area. Her family lived in

Whitesboro, Texas, just 20 miles east of Sherman, the county seat of Grayson County. She did not know any details of the lynching, but it was a disturbing memory that stuck with her all her life.

In April 2019 my wife, Susan, and I visited the National Memorial for Peace and Justice in Montgomery, Alabama. Also commonly known as the National Lynching Memorial, it was opened in 2018 as a memorial to the Black victims who were lynched in the United States. The memorial was developed by the Equal Justice Initiative, an organization founded by Bryan Stevenson. Stevenson is a lawyer who has challenged the bias against the poor and minorities found in criminal justice systems in America. He has worked on many cases saving prisoners from the death penalty by proving they were unjustly convicted. I highly recommend the 2019 movie *Just Mercy*, starring Michael B. Jordan. It tells the true story of how after graduating from Harvard, Bryan Stevenson moves to Alabama, where he starts a law practice targeting the defense of those wrongly convicted or the poor who cannot afford appropriate legal representation. The movie centers on one of his earliest cases, that of Walter McMillan, who is sentenced to die in 1987 for the murder of an 18-year-old girl, despite evidence proving his innocence. During the years of working on the case, Stevenson deals with racism and obstacles of legal and political maneuverings against his client.

The National Memorial for Peace and Justice is located on six acres in downtown Montgomery. In addition, the memorial is connected to the Legacy Museum: From Enslavement to Mass Incarceration. The Legacy Museum is located near the memorial on a historical site where enslaved people in Montgomery were bought and sold. The memorial and the museum tell the story of racial terror lynching, racial segregation, Jim Crow laws, and current problems of unjust arrests and police violence.

The six-acre site of the National Lynching Memorial includes sculptures, displays, and writings from Dr. Martin Luther King, Jr., and others. The largest part of the memorial is the centrally located square consisting of 805 six-foot hanging steel rectangles in the size and shape of coffins. Each of the six-foot beams represents a county within a state where racial terror lynching occurred verified by Equal Justice Initiative documentation. More than 4,075 documented lynchings of Black people took place between 1877 and 1950 and were concentrated in 12 Southern states. Each of the beams are engraved with the county and names of the lynching victims. The beams are distributed randomly, rather than being grouped by state. They are hung from the ceiling symbolic of how most lynching victims were subjected to hanging after initially being tortured.

The Memorial is a place of sadness and a place for lamentation. It is so well done and provides a large, quiet place to contemplate a very sad and regrettable part of our history. As Susan and I walked through the forest of hanging coffin-like structures we wanted to especially see the one for Grayson County, Texas, where my mother grew up and as a child overheard talk of a lynching. The following was engraved on the beam:

GRAYSON
COUNTY
TEXAS
JOHN MARTIN
06.26.1885
GEORGE HUGHES
05.09.1930

My mother was born in 1930, two months prior to the lynching of George Hughes. She probably heard the discussion of the lynching when she was four or five years old. It seems likely they were talking about the lynching of George Hughes, while recognizing it could have been another one in Texas or one that is not documented. I was never told the story of the lynching of George Hughes, but it was an infamous event in Grayson County.

The lynching of George Hughes was referred to as the "Sherman Riot," and it occurred approximately 20 miles from the farm where my mother grew up. George Hughes was a Black farmhand who was accused of raping a woman on a farm where he worked on May 3, 1930. He was arrested and indicted by a grand jury on May 5, 1930, and a trial date was set for Friday, May 9th. Police officers removed Hughes from the county jail to an undisclosed location to avoid possible mob violence from those who had been gathering around the jail. Early in the day on May 9th, the famous Texas Ranger, Frank Hamer, along with three other law enforcement officers, took Hughes to the Sherman County Courthouse. (In 1934 Frank Hamer would lead the posse who tracked down and killed criminals Bonnie Parker and Clyde Barrow.) Jury selection began that morning. No spectators were allowed in the courtroom, but a large crowd of people from all over the county gathered outside and later in the morning they began stoning the courthouse. The jury was sworn in at noon and when the first witness began testimony around 1:00 p.m., the crowd forced open the doors to the courtroom corridor. The Texas Rangers fired three warning shots and Hughes was taken and locked in the courthouse's walk-in-vault to protect him from the mob. The judge was reviewing finding another venue for the trial, but around 2:30 p.m. the mob threw an open can of gasoline into the county tax collector's office and set the building on fire. Court officials escaped the building by ladders and the mob attacked firemen and cut their hoses. Rangers were unable to rescue Hughes from the vault and Hughes suffocated and died locked inside. A detachment of national guardsman was sent but the mob forced them to retreat. The county courthouse completely burned down and all that was left was the concrete vault were Hughes had been taken. The mob used dynamite and acetylene torches on the vault and were able to open it around midnight. A crowd of more than 5,000 people raged in the courthouse yard and surrounding streets. The mob leaders tied Hughes's body behind a car and dragged it through the streets until they reached Sherman's Black commercial buildings. They hung Hughes's body from a tree and then mutilated it and partially burned it. Then the rioters looted and burned Black businesses and homes in the area. The following is from an article in the *New York Times* on May 11, 1930:

"At midnight the body of the Negro who had been burned to death in the vault was thrown down a ladder while the mob howled and cheered.

A parade was formed at once, with the body of Hughes on an automobile truck. Behind it marched several thousand hooting, yelling and jeering mean and boys. Women were among them with babes in their arms had been in the mob.

As the parade started someone yelled "Take him home," and the line swung toward the Negro section of the city, about seven or eight blocks distant. The body of Hughes was strung up to a tree in front of a two-story brick building containing a Negro drug store and rooming house. The drug store was broken into, and boxes, counters and other inflammable material brought out and piled under the hanging body. A torch was then applied.

After burning the body, the mob set fire to the drug store and to a number of other Negro homes and stores in a radius of three blocks, all being destroyed. Among these was the only Negro undertaking establishment in the city. A white undertaking firm had to be called to take charge of Hughes's body after it had been cut down by the militiamen."

The National Guard was called in on May 10th and Texas Governor Dan Moody declared martial law through May 24th. Fourteen suspects were indited on May 20th, but only one man was convicted of arson and one for rioting. No one was charged or punished for the lynching of George Hughes. In Nolan Thompson's account of the Sherman Riot, he said, "An American flag was carried around the grounds to incite the men to action."

The other name engraved on the lynching memorial for Grayson County, Texas, is John Martin. Martin was accused of being one of five people who murdered a Mrs. Hozell in Elkhart, Texas, in 1885. Martin left Elkhart the night of the murder and went to Bells, Texas, which is located about 15 miles east of Sherman. He awakened suspicion in Bells when upon his arrival he made an inquiry about the murder in Elkhart. A sheriff in Bells forwarded a description to Elkhart authorities who said, "it tallied exactly with the appearance of the man wanted." So based on this response from Elkhart, a Grayson County mob determined they would hang Martin at once. Newspaper reports said that the mob broke into the Bell's calaboose (the local jail) that night and "took him a short distance and strung him up."

After learning of these disturbing stories, I decided to research the names engraved in the lynching memorials for these other counties I have lived in:

- Dallas County, Texas
- Collin County, Texas
- White County, Arkansas

These are the names engraved on the beam for **Dallas County**:

DALLAS
COUNTY
TEXAS
WILLIAM TAYLOR
09.12.1884
HOLLAND BROOKS
03.03.1910

William Allen Taylor was arrested in early August of 1884 in Dallas for an alleged "dastardly assault" on Mrs. W. H. Flippen on June 22. He was being held in a Dallas jail, but in late August Sheriff Smith was fearful the jail would be attacked by a mob, so he quietly moved Taylor to the Waxahachie jail. People in Dallas found out Taylor had been moved and were planning to go and attack the jail in Waxahachie. Sherriff Smith got wind of the plans and on the night of September 11 he and Constable George Miller put Taylor in a double-seated buggy and headed towards Waco where they planned to put him in jail. Smith and Miller were tailed by nine men who then took the officers by surprise and disarmed them and "arrested" them. The nine men then took Taylor to an area one and a half miles west of Dallas where they were met by five hundred masked men. The mob quickly put a rope around Taylor's neck, and he was asked if he had anything to say. His last words were: "Boss, you're hanging an innocent man. I don't know anything about it and won't tell a lie by saying I do." Allen was handcuffed and hung to a tree. Newspaper accounts said he died hard and suffered for around 12 minutes. His body was not removed from the tree until the next day. The following quote was at the end of an article about the lynching that appeared in the *Fort Worth Daily Gazette* on September 13, 1884.

> *"The mob was quiet and orderly, saying not a word, but acting magnificently. The hanging was over an hour before it began to be noised about in the streets. One peculiarity about the mob was that it was comprised exclusively of boys under 21 years of age."*

On March 3, 1910, a 59-year-old handyman named Holland "Allen" Brooks was lynched by a white mob in downtown Dallas. Brooks was accused—without evidence—of assaulting his white employer's 2 ½ year old daughter. During a pretrial hearing for Mr. Brooks at the Dallas County Courthouse (known as the Old Red Courthouse), a mob of around 3,000 white men gathered and demanded Mr. Brooks be lynched. Members of the mob broke into the courtroom, seized Mr. Brooks from law enforcement officers, tied a rope around his neck, and threw him from the second-floor window of the courthouse, fracturing his skull upon impact. A separate faction of the mob surrounded Mr. Brooks, kicking and beating him before dragging him several blocks to the intersection of Main and Akard streets. The brutal, lawless violence continued near the Elks Arch, where Mr. Brooks was hanged from a telegraph pole in front of 5,000 onlookers. Photos of his lynched body were widely circulated, and postcards were published depicting the event. One postcard had this printed commentary on the back:

> *"This is a token of a great day we had in Dallas, March 3, a negro was hung for an assault on a three-year-old girl."*

Though several members of the mob gave newspaper interviews, no one was ever held responsible for the lynching of Allen Brooks. The site of this lynching was not marked until the Dallas County Justice Initiative placed a marker there in 2021.

These are the names engraved on the beam for **Collin County:**

COLLIN
COUNTY
TEXAS
COMMODORE JONES
08.11.1911

On August 11, 1911, in Farmersville, Texas, a young female telephone operator accused a Black man, Commodore Jones, of using insulting language to her over the telephone. The conversation upon which the complaint was based was overheard by others. A similar complaint was made a year earlier against Mr. Jones, but there were no witnesses, and the Grand Jury found no reason to prosecute him. The call was made from the residence of H. L. Carver where Mr. Jones lived. Mr. Jones had been an employee of Mr. Carver for several years and Mr. Carter considered him a trustworthy person. Mr. Jones was arrested by Constable Wisdom and his plan was to take him to McKinney, Texas, the county seat. Constable Wisdom missed the train to McKinney but was able to place Mr. Jones in the local jail as he made his way through a mob of about 300 people. A Sherriff Robinson came over from McKinney to take Mr. Jones but he returned home without him because of threats made to him by the Farmersville mob. A crowd of about 75 men and boys gained entrance into the Farmersville jail and then marched Mr. Jones to the public square where they forced him to climb a telephone pole. There was a member of the mob waiting at the top of the pole and he threw a rope around Mr. Jones's neck, and Jones was forced to jump. He soon strangled to death.

These are the names engraved on the beam for **White County**:

WHITE
COUNTY
ARKANSAS
JAMES BAILEY
07.08.1891
S.A. JENKINS
05.24.1900
UNKNOWN
07.05.1910

Based upon the 1880 census, a James Bailey lived in White County Arkansas who was 5 years old. This means in 1891 Bailey would have been just 16 years old. According to the *Arkansas Gazette,* on the evening of July 7, 1891, the ladies of the Methodist Church in Beebe, Arkansas, had a social gathering and lawn festival near the church. Bailey was seen loitering around the grove where the festival was held and was described as a "town loafer." A thunderstorm rolled through around 9:30 p.m. and the gathering ended, so people started walking home in the dark. Mrs. Folsom left for home accompanied by the 13-year-old daughter of Mr. J. F. Bass. As they were quickly walking home in the dark, they collided with James Bailey. He grabbed the young girl's shoulder and accused her of trying to push him off the sidewalk. Bailey then allegedly caught Mrs. Folsom, knocked her down, and "brutally outraged her person." She reported the assault and said her purse had been stolen.

Baily was arrested on the morning of July 8th and appeared before a Justice of the Peace. He denied assaulting Folsom and her purse had already been found nearby, so he was released. Later that morning, Folsom decided she needed to see a doctor and told him about the assault. Word of this spread fast through Beebe and a large, mounted posse of around 500 gathered, incentivized by a $125 reward. He was caught around 3:00 p.m. near Garner, Arkansas. Local Blacks formed a mob of around 30 with plans to take Bailey from the posse. In response to that threat, a couple of leaders of the white mob took a path through the woods and returned Bailey to the jail. Later that night a white mob removed Bailey from the jail, and he was hung from a railroad crossing sign.

S. A. Jenkins was a Black school teacher in West Point, Arkansas, located about 9 miles southeast of Searcy, the seat of White County. On the evening of Saturday, May 23, 1900, in West Point, two places of business were broken into. On Sunday night, two white men called out two black men, Mr. Jenkins and Mr. Durham. The white men told Jenkins and Durham they were under arrest and proceeded to take them into town. Jenkins and Durham asked to see the warrants for their arrest, but they were told they would have to wait until they got into town. On their way, several more white men jumped out with shotguns aimed at them at an attempt to frighten them into confessing. Jenkins started to run and one of the white men shot him in the back, killing him. The men then tried unsuccessfully to get Durham to confess, and they let him go. The article in the Arkansas Gazette described the event as more "whitecapping" (or nightriding) than lynching. The term whitecapping covered a variety of vigilante practices typically done by white men in disguise and usually under the cover of darkness. Cases of whitecapping are typically included in the tabulations of lynching victims in America.

The Equal Justice Initiative found that most terror lynchings can best be understood as having the features of one or more of the following:[49]

- Lynchings that resulted from a wildly distorted fear of interracial sex
- Lynchings in response to casual social transgressions
- Lynchings based upon allegations of serious violent crime
- Public spectacle lynchings
- Lynchings that escalated into large-scale violence targeting the entire African American community
- Lynchings of sharecroppers, ministers, and community leaders who resisted mistreatment, which were most common between 1915 and 1940

After the Civil War the Southern States amended their constitutions to restrict the voting rights of Black citizens. In addition, amendments were passed prohibiting interracial marriage and requiring the segregation of the public schools. State and local laws were passed designed to uphold the notion of white supremacy and to oppress Black people. These are commonly called the "Jim Crow System." Jim Crow laws focused on keeping Blacks and whites apart. Here are some examples of this segregation system:

- Black people were not allowed to use public libraries

- Separate Black and white restrooms, drinking fountains, and waiting rooms

- Many restaurants refused to serve Black people or they might have to use a back entrance to be served

- At the Texas State Fair, Black people could only attend on one day that was specifically designated for them

- Black people had to sit in the balconies of movie theaters or go to "Black Only" theaters

- They had to ride in the back of public buses

White people rarely showed Blacks common courtesy and could harass, threaten, beat or even kill Black individuals with little fear of punishment. The legal system was stacked against the Black population—all the judges were white and almost all juries were white. In many jurisdictions, Black individuals were not allowed to testify against whites in trials.

The Jim Crow era of segregation was said to have ended when Congress in bipartisan fashion overcame Southern filibusters to pass the Civil Rights Act of 1964 and the Voting Rights Act of 1965. This was an improvement, but it did not end many practices of segregation and white supremacy.

It's hard to look at the recorded stories of the lynchings of Black people that took place in the counties where I have lived—let alone the more than 4,000 addition lynchings that took place in the South. But we need to have the courage to accept and acknowledge history and not ignore these events just because they make us "feel bad" or pretend those events have not had an effect on our society today.

In her book, *Be the Bridge,* Latasha Morrison says this about "LAMENT."

> *"What is the purpose of lament? It allows us to connect with and grieve the reality of our sin and suffering. It draws us to repentant connection with God in that suffering. Lament also serves as an effort to change God's mind, to ask him to turn things around in our favor. Lament seeks God as comforter, healer, restorer, and redeemer. Somehow the act of lament reconnects us with God and leads to hope and redemption.*
>
> *But it's no secret that we as a culture are uncomfortable with lament. Rarely do we look to share our pain publicly. In fact, we are encouraged to mourn quietly and in private...author and professor Soong-Chan Rah relates our avoidance of lament to a culture of triumphalism. He wrote that, as Americans, we love to focus on praise, comfort, thanksgiving, and worship—anything but lament"*[50]

January 6, 2021, was a sad day for me. That morning, I received a call from my brother telling me our mother had passed away. She had been in hospice care and memory care for a relatively long time. So, that was not really a time of lamentation. It was a time to celebrate 90 years of a life well-lived and for the grace of her not being in hospice memory care any longer.

But in addition, the rioting mob attack on the U.S. Capitol on January 6, 2021, was a sad day for America. The stories I have recalled of the lynching mobs attacking the law enforcement officers in past history are prophetic. The mob attack was not something new in this country. America is not a Christian nation. America is a violent nation. We need to confess, lament, spend some time in sorrow, and repent.

The following are the words of King David after spending time in lamentation about his sins:

Psalm 51:10-17 (NIV)

[10] Create in me a pure heart, O God,

and renew a steadfast spirit within me.

[11] Do not cast me from your presence

or take your Holy Spirit from me.

[12] Restore to me the joy of your salvation

and grant me a willing spirit, to sustain me.

[13] Then I will teach transgressors your ways,

so that sinners will turn back to you.

[14] Deliver me from the guilt of bloodshed, O God,

you who are God my Savior,

and my tongue will sing of your righteousness.

[15] Open my lips, Lord,

and my mouth will declare your praise.

[16] You do not delight in sacrifice, or I would bring it;

you do not take pleasure in burnt offerings.

[17] My sacrifice, O God, is[a broken spirit;

a broken and contrite heart

you, God, will not despise.

Chapter 13

IN THE YEAR 2020

Littleton Church of Christ
June 11, 2020

In early 2020, Jovan Barrington, the preaching minister of the Littleton Church of Christ, began a sermon series called "My Skin: Racial Reconciliation." It was the first and only sermon series I heard in a Church of Christ dealing with the issue of racism. Jovan's father was of white European descent and his mother was from Panama, a descendent of African and Spanish inhabitants of the Caribbean. Jovan was born in Panama, but grew up in Dothan, Alabama. While Jovan's genealogical heritage is diverse, he said that in Alabama if a policeman stopped him and told him to get his Black "a**" out the car, he did not argue with him. Jovan's wonderful wife, Ana, is Black and grew up in the Dominican Republic. Jovan had been the lead minister of the Littleton Church of Christ, a predominantly white congregation, for about 4 ½ years when he began the sermon series on race reconciliation.

My wife Susan and I were married in 1974 and attended our first church service as a married couple at the Prestoncrest Church of Christ in North Dallas. Prestoncrest was a new "church plant" and had around 200 members at the time we placed membership. Susan had grown up at the Walnut Hill Church of Christ in Dallas, and I grew up at the Richardson East Church of Christ (formerly Abrams Road). Both of our parents still attended those churches, so we decided it would be good for us to start our marriage at a new church together. We were members at Prestoncrest for almost 27 years until we moved to Denver, Colorado, in 2001. Our two daughters, Amy and Katy, were baptized in that church and I served as an "Elder" and Susan served as an "Elder's Wife" for more than five years. Prestoncrest was an integrated congregation. Our minister, Prentice Meador, was an advocate of racial equality. We would have guest Black preachers present sermons on Sunday mornings at least once or twice a year. However, Prestoncrest did not formally cooperate or collaborate with Black churches. (Also, we did not collaborate much with other white Churches—unless they were overseas.) The Prestoncrest church grew rapidly over the years, and by the late 1990s it had a membership of more than 1,600 people. While we considered ourselves an integrated congregation, in reality, we had a very small percentage of Black members. I looked at the 1998 pictorial Prestoncrest Church Directory and counted around 1650 total members—24 of those members were Black—1.5% of the total membership. A majority of those Black members were very involved and a positive influence on that congregation. The most influential Black member of the Prestoncrest Church was Theresa Simpson. Theresa lived in Hamilton Park, the area of Dallas I referred to in an earlier chapter. Theresa became a widow around 1990 and attended church with her mother Naomi. Her daughter, Barbara, (who became the lead administrative assistant in the church office) and son-in-law also were members. Theresa would sit in the second row of pews in the sanctuary and was always dressed in her Sunday best. Prentice Meador was a talented and intense speaker who could bring good sermons on Sunday. Prentice and Theresa made a dynamic tandem. The overall worship service at Prestoncrest was very traditional and completely male-dominated. Granted, 1,000 people singing a capella can be pretty moving given the right hymn, but the worship dynamic was intentionally cerebral and lacking emotion. However, when it came to Prentice bringing an intellectual sermon—Theresa brought the Black American church tradition into play at Prestoncrest. She brought feeling to the sermon as she added verbal celebration to the hearing of the Word of God. She would participate by saying out loud with compassion:

"Oh, that's right."

"Preach it, Brother."

"Praise God."

"Thank you, Jesus."

And after a challenging point:

"Huuummmmm."

Teresa would also be involved with the public prayers by adding a "Yes, Lord," to certain petitions. So, Teresa made Prentice Meador's sermons better and brought some valuable Black church traditions to our services.

However, I believe this made this 98.5% white church feel it was less segregated than it really was. It made us oblivious to the racial issues all around us in Dallas County. Teresa was a blessing—but her example should have spurred us on to be more sensitive, introspective, and more aware of social justice issues.

Jovan's sermons on race reconciliation were very kind, gentle, and somewhat of an introduction on how to talk about something everyone did not talk about. The Littleton Church of Christ had a small but active number of Black members and the Board of Elders had at least one Black person in that group for several years. But, like the Prestoncrest congregation, the Littleton Church of Christ congregation was probably more than 90% white. The white majority had not been asking for a sermon series on race relations. Like most white Christians who had been living in the white nationalist bubble of America—they thought everything was fine. I mean, Barack Obama had been elected as President of the United States. I was grateful Jovan had the courage to take this subject on but in mid-March of 2020 the State of Colorado shut down most public gatherings because of the COVID-19 outbreak. So, the church services of the Littleton Church of Christ pivoted to online gatherings, and the sermon series on race relations was not continued.

In the spring of 2001 Susan and I made a trip to Colorado to look for a home in southeast Denver. I had accepted a job with United Dominion Realty Trust (UDR), a public company investing in multi-family apartment complexes. One evening during that house-hunting trip I set out to drive by the Littleton Church of Christ. We heard about the Littleton church from a couple who attended the Prestoncrest church in Dallas. Their adult son had been critically injured a skiing accident that left him significantly paralyzed, and the Littleton church had reached out to help them and their son during a very difficult time. (Susan later volunteered to stay with this young man one day every week when it was too dangerous for him to be alone.) This was before the invention of the iPhone, and I was using a rudimentary navigation system in our rental car to guide me over to the Littleton church building. Although I got close, I never found the church building that night. The navigation system took me to a funeral home on Colorado Blvd., but I did not see that the church building was next door. The building at the time was set far back from the road and there were no lights on the building. The church sign was an old rock engraved with what I would call art deco-type script lettering from the 1960s that simply said, Church of Christ. In addition, the unlighted sign was located parallel to Colorado Blvd, so you could not read it as you were driving down the street. After we had been members at Littleton for a few months I suggested to leadership that a new sign should be put up that would be more inviting and easier for new visitors to find. It would be several years before that sign was changed.

On May 25, 2020, Mr. George Floyd died after being handcuffed and pinned to the ground by Minneapolis police officers. The episode was captured on video, and it touched off national protests during the COVID-19 pandemic. Significant protests happened in downtown Denver shortly after Floyd's death. It is important to know that approximately 9 months earlier on August 24, 2019, three Aurora, Colorado, police officers confronted Mr. Elijah Jovan McClain, a 23-year-old man from Aurora as he was walking unarmed back to his house after buying some snacks from a convenience store. McClain was forcibly held to the ground with his hands cuffed behind his back and a police officer put him in a choke hold two times. Paramedics subsequently administered ketamine (later determined to be more than a therapeutic dosage) to McClain to sedate him. While on scene McClain went into cardiac arrest. Three days after arriving at the hospital, he was declared brain dead, and was removed from life support on August 30, 2019.

Around 2018, the Littleton Church did some upgrades on the church building and one of the renovations was the addition of a new church sign. The new digital screen could display multiple messages, pictures, colors, and even the time and temperature. It was a big purchase, but I personally thought it would be helpful to reach our neighbors in a nonintrusive way as they drove by. Drivers could see worship times, food bank hours, VBS dates, etc., and get a sense of what the church was about.

On June 10, 2020, Jovan Barrington came over to our house to sit with me on the back porch, in the open air, more than six feet apart to talk about how he was coping with the challenges of doing ministry during the COVID-19 shutdown. The church was still grieving the loss of Mike Myers, who died in April due to complications from COVID-19. Mike served the Littleton church for 49 years as a youth minister and lead minister and was a beloved pastor and mentor to many, including Jovan. We discussed issues of racism and how the church could do better in this area. As we ended our discussion, we stood up and started to walk to the front of the house. I stopped walking, a sudden thought hitting me out of the blue. I turned and said to Jovan, "You know what we should do? We should put 'Black Lives Matter' on the church sign." It seemed logical considering our congregation's discussions about racial reconciliation and having Black leaders as part of our leadership. Jovan said he thought it would be appropriate and he would consider it. I then suggested maybe he should "run that by the Elders," but he said they did not require him to get their approval for content put on the sign. He then left and I figured probably "Black Lives Matter" would not be added to the current scroll of messages. We lived about a mile from the church and the next morning I drove by the sign and as I noted the "time and temperature" the next image on the sign was "BLACK LIVES MATTER." I was surprised and happy at the same time. After 202 years from the time when the young minister, Moses Mackoy, was forced to stop teaching literacy to Black enslaved people so that they could read the Bible—a Church of Christ stepped forward and made a simple affirmation for racial reconciliation. That evening around dusk, I went and took a photograph of the church sign under the shadow of the cross that is on the very top of the Littleton church building.

Our neighbors, a husband and wife who were the same age as us, who live across the street, mentioned on several occasions they would like to visit our church. We invited them to go with us from time to time, but it never worked out. Later that day, Susan received a long text rant from the wife saying the church had done a terrible thing by posting that "Black Lives Matter" on the sign. I talked with her on the phone, and she said that we were backing the official manifesto of the "Black Lives Matter" formal organization, and they were out to destroy America and that "all lives matter." The conversation did not go well as, I tried to point out that grammatically we could have said "BLACK LIVES MATTER, TOO" but if whites were aware of the history of the terrible treatment of Blacks in America, then we could be less fragile in our sensitivity to what is essentially a minor grammatical error. The conversation moved to her statement that President Trump was chosen by God, and we then agreed to disagree.

"For instance, some Christians question the Americanness of any-one protesting under the banner of Black Lives Matter. In the next breath, they might hint at how these protests call into question

how anyone associated with this group could be aligned with God's desires...The key factor is clearly highlighting who "we" are not. This is the quickest and easiest way to define who "we" are for or what features define 'us'. Christian nationalist rhetoric consistently resorts to demonizing the 'other". .... Andrew L. Whitehead[51]

The Littleton church received a few calls from neighbors expressing their objection to the sign. Several church members stated that "All Lives Matter" and the message should be deleted, and a few members even left to attend other churches. The Littleton Church elders, or shepherds, did not ask the message be removed from the sign, but they did send the following letter to the congregation a week later:

June 18, 2020

Statement regarding "Black Lives Matter" and the Littleton Church of Christ

As elders we feel compelled by love to comment on the killing of George Floyd and others as it relates to our church family. As with any family, some conversations are difficult. Emotions run high as we see protests throughout our country, these make it difficult to really listen to one another. We're asking our family to listen to one another with the confidence that comes from the love of Christ.

We are convinced that every human being is made in the image of GOD, and Christ died and rose again for all humanity. We live in a country founded on this basic principle: "We hold these truths to be self-evident, that all men are created equal, that they are endowed by their Creator with certain unalienable rights..." (The Declaration of Independence). It is important our conversations are based on the higher truths of equality and justice; not the lesser kind of right versus left that only polarizes people.

While we are not endorsing "Black Lives Matter" as a platform, our conviction is that black lives matter. It is a conviction born out of love, caring, and concern for people of color not from an alignment with political ideologies. We believe every live matters as much as every other life, regardless of ethnicity. It is for this reason we stand in solidarity with those who seek equal justice under the law for black citizens who have historically and continually been deprived of their "unalienable rights."

Our vision statement talks about reaching the next generation for Christ, so unless we lean into racial healing in our nation, our church, our community, we will lose credibility with a generation that is far out in front of us on this issue. In times like this we believe the church should work for equal justice, racial healing and reconciliation. Therefore, we have decided to use "Black Lives Matter" on our sign and social media posts as a statement of fact born out of our desire to "Love God and Go Love People."

To further raise awareness and promote understanding of racism and to take action against it, the staff and the shepherds are studying "Be the Bridge: Pursuing God's Heart for Racial Reconciliation" by Latasha Morrison. We have made a $500 donation to Be the Bridge nonprofit organization for the purposes of supporting their efforts to educated churches and facilitate reconciliation groups.

We want to hear from you to address your questions and concerns. We believe that each of you desires to "love your neighbor as yourself" and cares deeply about what happens in this country, so we appeal to you to join us in working for the common good. We love each of you with the love of Christ and desire to walk with you on a journey of understanding and healing.

Grace and peace,

The Littleton Church Shepherds

The Black Lives Matters sign ran for a couple of weeks after this letter went out and then it was taken out of the rotation. The letter sent out by the elders probably elicited more discussion than the sign. Some thought the letter went too far and some thought it did not go far enough. At least the conversations were happening, rather than the typical "radio silence" existing at most churches. I recently asked one of the elders, who is Black, what he thought when he first saw the "Black Lives Matter" on the church sign. He said, "I just felt happy that *my* church would do that."

Some white church members responded with "All Lives Matter" on Jovan Barrington's social media when he posted my photograph of the sign. I would characterize the negative comments expressed as showing a lack of empathy and understanding of systemic racism.

I posted my photograph of the church sign on Facebook and received about 20 likes and a kind affirmation from a former Black member of our church. Six days after that Facebook post I received an email from my 93-year-old father in Dallas. It was a reply to my email checking to see if he had received any tax information on an annuity that I was trying to help him obtain. He had a Facebook account he used to follow family news. His brief response included a rare piece of advice for me:

June 27, 2020

Have not received.

P.S. A little father advice. Don't get involved in the black man matter mess.

Dad

The legacy of John B. Floyd lives on.

Chapter 14

BLIND SPOTS

The most significant surprise in my search of my family history was the finding of the genealogical study done in 1931 by Cousin Mabel Lee Mackoy, 92 years ago, before the invention of the word processor, the internet, and Ancestry.com. She traced my family roots all the way back to 1619 and the origin of slavery in America. This finding was the tipping point for me to pursue the writing of this book. On June 15, 2021, the Texas Legislature passed House Bill No. 3979 that placed restrictions on the social studies curriculum in public schools. The following are some excerpts from that bill:

> *"For any social studies course in the required curriculum: ...*
>
> *4) a teacher, administrator, or other employee of state agency, school district, or open—enrollment charter school may not: ...*
>
> *(B) require or make part of a course the concept that:*
>
> *vi) an individual, by virtue of the individual's race or sex, bears responsibility for actions committed in the past by other members of the same race or sex;*
>
> *vii) an individual should feel discomfort, guilt, anguish, or any other form of psychological stress on account of the individual's race or sex;*

viii) meritocracy or traits such as hard work ethic are racist or sexist or were created by members of a particular race to oppress members of another race;

(ix) the advent of slavery in the territory of the United States constituted the true founding of the United States; or

(x) with respect to their relationships to American values, slavery and racism are anything other than deviations from, betrayals of, or failures to live up to, the authentic founding principles of the United States, which include liberty and equality; and

(C) require an understanding of the 1619 project

So, in Texas, it is permissible to read about what Mabel Lee Mackoy said about your families' ties to 1619—just make sure you don't understand what it might mean in relation to your family history. What are some of the "authentic founding principles" of the United States?

- Black people can be enslaved and count for only 60% of a person
- Black people have no legal right to marry and keep their families together
- Women are not allowed to vote
- Indigenous people are not allowed to be United States citizens

Like it or not, the United States' founding fathers included slavery as part of its true founding. It's interesting this Texas law does not address the "founding principles of the Constitution of the Republic of Texas." In 1836, the Texas constitution contained these principles:

- All persons of color who were slaves for life before their emigration to Texas shall remain slaves.
- The Texas Congress does not have power to emancipate slaves.
- Africans, the descendants of Africans and Indians cannot be considered citizens of the Republic.
- Women were not allowed to vote.

Is it "legal" to read the Constitution of the Republic of Texas in public schools? The esteemed Texas Legislature seemed to have forgotten that Texas was once its own Republic. Maybe it would have caused them to *"feel discomfort, guilt, anguish, or any other form of psychological stress."*

When I learned of my family's direct connection to the establishment of slavery in Virginia in 1619, I felt discomfort, guilt, and some anguish. But, as a privileged white male sitting in my home office in Lone Tree, Colorado, was I feeling stress? I think the "stress" referred to in the Texas law really means experiencing "white fragility." They don't want to get their feelings hurt. As a white American, I need to learn from "The Mabel Lee Mackoy 1619 Project" and own up to both the known and unknown biases I have. I need to confess to what Beth Moore has referred to as our "ancient hostilities."

During most of my life, I was taught what is said in House Bill No. 3979: *Slavery and racism were just: deviations or failures to live up to the "Founding Principles of the United States."* However, I learned in this journey through my family's history this could not be farther from the truth. "White Supremacy" and the right for white people to own Black people was clearly debated, litigated, and codified into state laws and constitutions. The Virginia code of 1705 said that Black, Mulatto, and Indian slaves "shall be held to be real estate." In 1792, the constitution of the State of Kentucky stated that the slavery laws of Virginia were in force in Kentucky. Slavery and White Supremacy were without a doubt, key founding principles of the United States. When Texas was part of Mexico, Black people were free. When Texas became an independent Republic, the principle of slavery was clearly articulated in its new constitution. Slavery was a founding principle of the Republic of Texas.

"Fragile white people" like to say: "I'm not racist…racism ended when slavery ended." Even a casual look at history in America after the Civil War proves this statement to be ludicrous. During the Jim Crow era Blacks were socially and economically marginalized—and brutally lynched by whites. I attended segregated schools until 1968. Racism did not end when slavery was abolished, rather, it flourished in America.

The examination of my family tree revealed that my ancestors, on both sides of my family, owned slaves. These same ancestors put the Christian church as a top priority in their lives and earnestly sought to "restore" the ancient Christian faith back to the practices of the first century. This is a "Profound Contradiction." So how could my Christian ancestors arrive at the position that it was morally acceptable to buy, own and sell other people?

They Believed in White Supremacy

The United States was founded by Europeans who believed that they were part of a "pure" white race, and they had the God-given right to maintain power over American Indigenous people and Black people who had been kidnapped from Africa. They created the false hierarchy putting light-skinned Europeans at the top with unlimited privilege and political power. They believed they had the God-given right to use violence to protect their power and prevent them from any resistance from the people they conquered or enslaved. White Supremacy flourished from 1619 forward and was a fully formed systemic part of American society when the Stone/Campbell church movement began 200 years ago.

The Practice of American Idolatry—Christian Nationalism

My forefathers believed the myth that the United States was a Christian nation, and the Constitution was divinely inspired. However, John B. Floyd bent the teachings of Jesus and the Bible to conform to the existing laws of the United States Constitution. However, they were unwilling to accept the democratic election of Abraham Lincoln—because they believed the Constitution gave them the right to own slaves.

The Failure to see the "Systemic Sin" of the Peculiar Institution

The Peculiar Institution, slavery, was systemic in American thought and everyday life. The concept of White Supremacy had been normalized and the Europeans who immigrated to America did not consider Indigenous Americans or Black people as fully human. When Moses Mackoy started his underground literacy school for Black people in 1818, White Supremacy and slavery had been practiced and legalized for 200 years in America. Slavery was considered a normal social system enjoying a nostalgic type of appreciation by white people. The Texas Legislature banned the critical study of the history of racism and the 1619 Project because they believe that racism is just an inter-personal issue—not something that is imbedded in American laws and daily norms. Please listen to this: systematic sin exists and is present in a larger social context. My American ancestors (along with us) were immersed in a highly individualistic world view. This individuality mindset has invaded Christian thought and practice— "Jesus is my personal Savior, and it's between me and Him." It can be very difficult at times to recognize corporate, systematic sin— especially from a white person who is benefited by the institution of slavery or is someone who is not personally affected. The persecuted slaves had no voice, and the poor today have no voice. My ancestors were blind to the systematic oppression of slavery.

Biblical Legalism

This pursuit of "restoration" was compromised by a legalistic reading of the Bible. While they believed in the Trinity—God the Father, God the Son, God the Holy Spirit—in effect, they added the Holy Bible as a "fourth addition" to the Trinity. They wanted to follow the Bible as their only guide: "Speak where the Bible speaks and be silent where the Bible is silent." This approach led to a legalistic view of Christianity, much like the Pharisees in the time of Jesus' ministry. The Pharisees were very strict in their rules regarding the observance of the Sabbath on the seventh day of the week, and they thought Jesus was far too liberal in his approach to the Sabbath day. The following is an account of Jesus dealing with the Pharisees:

> [9] *Going on from that place, he went into their synagogue,* [10] *and a man with a shriveled hand was there. Looking for a reason to bring charges against Jesus, they asked him, "Is it lawful to heal on the Sabbath?"* [11] *He said to them, "If any of you has a sheep and it falls into a pit on the Sabbath, will you not take hold of*

*it and lift it out? ^{12} How much more valuable is a person than a
sheep! Therefore, it is lawful to do good on the Sabbath."^{13} Then
he said to the man, "Stretch out your hand." So he stretched it out
and it was completely restored, just as sound as the other. ^{14} But the
Pharisees went out and plotted how they might kill Jesus.*

—Matthew 12:9-14 NIV

It's as though Jesus is saying, "Use your common sense." If you act from love,
you will help a sick person or a lamb in distress on the Sabbath, but instead,
the Pharisees were legalistic in their approach. When Barton W. Stone saw the
harsh treatment of slaves near Charleston, his "soul was sickened at the sight of
slavery," and he immediately knew it was wrong. He did not go find some proof
text out of the Old Testament, politics, or—like Alexander Campbell—say
he could not find a specific prohibition spelled out in the Bible. Jesus stated it
simply when He was asked what the greatest commandments are:

*^{35} One of them, an expert in the law, tested him with this ques-
tion: ^{36} "Teacher, which is the greatest commandment in the
Law?"^{37} Jesus replied: "'Love the Lord your God with all your heart
and with all your soul and with all your mind.' ^{38} This is the first
and greatest commandment. ^{39} And the second is like it: 'Love your
neighbor as yourself.' ^{40} All the Law and the Prophets hang on these
two commandments."*

—Matthew 22:35-40 NIV

Love your neighbor as yourself. It's a no-brainer. Slavery is wrong.

Preservation of Economic Wealth

I believe that money, money, money—the fear of losing economic wealth—was
a contributing factor for wanting to keep the institution of slavery. This would
often be referred to as the romanticized lament that the "Southern Way of
Life" would be lost. The loss of free labor would decrease the profits in cotton
and other agricultural industries. Whites would have less time to relax on the

porch and, since Black people could no longer be sold for cash, and the net worth of white people would drop significantly.

The temptation is to throw my forefathers under the bus and pretend I am not infected by these old practices and thoughts. However, the reality is these ancestral blind spots are not extinct. They are like a virus continually mutating into variants fogging my vision and distorting my perceptions. So, what is the "vaccine" for these blind spots? It is not pretending we are not sick—believing if we can read a few large letters at the top of the eye chart we can see well enough. We can't just "yada, yada" the fine print. Often, a vaccination can make us feel uncomfortable for a while, but the medicine wakes up our immune systems and the body prepares itself for potentially harmful outside influences. We need to not just listen to things that we almost automatically agree with and even give us a dopamine hit of affirmation. We need a dose of humility, confession, and love—and expect this may cause us at times to feel uncomfortable. We need to move from simplistic belief to faith. A faith that doubts, confesses, and ultimately trusts and loves.

We live in a society where the pendulum of thinking goes from one extreme to another. We offer no room for nuance or empathy for others who are not like us. Christianity must be associated with love and grace along with social justice. Everything cannot simplistically be reduced to "liberal" or "conservative." We need to see gray in a world of black and white.

I sometimes wonder what blind spots my future great-grandchildren will see that I had. I could list several, but I have chosen to discuss one in particular that makes me uncomfortable when I contemplate it. And it is probably the most important doctrine of the United States: capitalism.

I am a classically educated and trained capitalist. I obtained an accounting degree from Harding College and was a member of Harding's American Studies program. The program's purpose was to expose about 50 students to people promoting a better understanding of capitalism and free enterprise. We made trips to St. Louis, Chicago, New Orleans, and Dallas, where we toured businesses and met with people like Chicago's Mayor Richard Daley and even Tom Landry of the Dallas Cowboys. I also was a member of the five-person Harding College Business team that competed in the Emory University Business Game held in Atlanta in 1972. It was a six-week competition between 40 colleges and universities from Southern, Midwestern, and Eastern Seaboard States. The competition was divided into five separate divisions with eight schools competing in each division. The teams theoretically manufactured and sold stainless steel flatware and household products. Managerial decisions were made by the teams for each business quarter and sent to the Emory Business School that used a computer program to process the results of the business simulation game. The Harding team went to Atlanta at the end of the six weeks and made presentations of our strategy (via overhead projector) and answered questions from a panel of experienced business professionals. The Harding team won its eight-team division and progressed to the "Final Five" part of the competition, where the teams gave another presentation and defense of their strategy and business plan. The final five schools were: Notre Dame, Marshall University, University of Kentucky, Brandeis University, and Harding College. The Harding College Business team won the competition and became the first school to win the Emory competition twice. While I am biased, I believe Harding College had one of the best business schools in the country in 1972. Upon graduation, I was well-prepared to go to work at a Dallas CPA firm and pass the CPA exam. In addition to all the business courses I took at Harding, I also benefited from my required liberal arts classes. I had enough hours in Bible classes to qualify as a minor with my degree.

However, the "gospel" taught at Harding went beyond the typical Bible courses. I believe it is fair to say that part of the gospel taught at Harding was "American Capitalism" and "The Free Enterprise System." The 2009 Michael Moore film *Capitalism: A Love Story* includes a clip from an old National Education Program Film that features former Harding College president Cliff Ganus saying this:

> *"We know that "American Capitalism" is morally right because*
> *its chief elements: private ownership, the profit motive, and the*

*competitive market are wholesome and good. They are compatible
with God's laws and the teachings of the Bible."*

The statement above was generally the mindset I operated from during most
of my business career. It should be noted the "pay gap" was much more equi-
table when this film was distributed more than 50 years ago. Now, however,
based upon my life experience, I'm seeing a lot of gray in this view of American
Capitalism. Private ownership is maybe good if you have an oil well hit on
your small 75-acre farm, but not so good if you are Black and deprived of the
right to acquire a small farm. Thankfully our national parks have not fallen
into private hands. Maximizing profits that prevent ordinary citizens from
receiving healthcare or not sharing profits with the labors who help produce
the profits does not seem wholesome. Cutthroat competition that eliminates
people's jobs without any kind of safety net strikes me as anything but good.
I could go on, but I think you get the picture.

Capitalism does not appear to be "black and white" in this passage from
the New Testament:

> *[42] They devoted themselves to the apostles' teaching and to fellowship,
> to the breaking of bread and to prayer. [43] Everyone was filled with
> awe at the many wonders and signs performed by the apostles. [44] All
> the believers were together and had everything in common. [45] They
> sold property and possessions to give to anyone who had need. [46] Every
> day they continued to meet together in the temple courts. They
> broke bread in their homes and ate together with glad and sincere
> hearts, [47] praising God and enjoying the favor of all the people. And
> the Lord added to their number daily those who were being saved.*
>
> *—Acts 2:42-47 NIV*

Here is another challenging passage that begins with this question:

> *[16] Just then a man came up to Jesus and asked, "Teacher, what good
> thing must I do to get eternal life?"...Matthew 19:16 NIV*

Jesus could have replied, "Maximize profits." However, that is *not* what Jesus said. Here is the answer Jesus gave:

> [17] *"Why do you ask me about what is good?" Jesus replied. "There is only One who is good. If you want to enter life, keep the commandments."* [18] *"Which ones?" he inquired. Jesus replied, "'You shall not murder, you shall not commit adultery, you shall not steal, you shall not give false testimony,* [19] *honor your father and mother,' and 'love your neighbor as yourself.']* [20] *"All these I have kept," the young man said. "What do I still lack?"* [21] *Jesus answered, "If you want to be perfect, go, sell your possessions and give to the poor, and you will have treasure in heaven. Then come, follow me."* [22] *When the young man heard this, he went away sad, because he had great wealth.* [23] *Then Jesus said to his disciples, "Truly I tell you, it is hard for someone who is rich to enter the kingdom of heaven.* [24] *Again I tell you, it is easier for a camel to go through the eye of a needle than for someone who is rich to enter the kingdom of God."*

> —*Matthew 19:17-24 NIV*

I was appropriately taught in church and at Harding College to give as we have been prospered to church and charitable causes. But the fear of "communism" has dominated the discussion, rather than the discussion of social equity and the needs of the poor. The major cause of poverty is systemic and cannot be solved solely by church tithes.

I would hope that Christian schools like Harding University, Abilene Christian University, and Pepperdine University would initiate studies of capitalism and how it can be better used with Christian values. My hope is they would engage in studies to deal with homeless populations, affordable housing, making healthcare more affordable, a better understanding of modern money theory, excessive profits, consumerism, extreme income gaps, etc. Simplistic "Dave Ramsey" classes conducted in a lot of churches are not addressing the fundamental challenges given to us in the teachings of Jesus regarding caring for the poor and marginalized.

Jesus spoke of an economy based upon love for your neighbor and cautioned his disciples to not see things through a lens of scarcity that leads to hoarding and fear. Love seeks abundance for others. Love makes a market "free."

A lot more needs to be discussed regarding the blind spot of capitalism, but I wanted to use it as an example of a blind spot my descendants will say I had.

Like my forefathers, I also have blind spots. I hope that I can see glimpses of those mindsets and realize that pride, tradition, and fear can prevent me from testing my settled beliefs.

As I am writing this in late October of 2023 a mass shooter killed at least 18 people in Maine. The continued tolerance of gun violence in America is a tragic blind spot. The vaguely written Second Amendment to the United States Constitution is not a divine law that cannot be changed.

Conclusion

We live in an amazing time when ordinary people have relatively affordable access to almost all the historical documents that have existed since time began. I am amazed at the access to historical newspapers, books, genealogies, census records, academic papers, letters, etc., that can be called up on a computer screen or obtained by a next-day Amazon delivery. There has never been a time when so much historical information has been so readily available. I have learned things about my third-great-grandfathers that my own grandparents did not know. *Newspapers.com* was not available in their lifetime. It is a unique and remarkable time for me to make this journey.

I have come to realize that these stories about churches and race relations are not "ancient history." I recently was talking with a friend, and he told me that his mother's father lived to be 105 years old. He knew him as a child and remembered that he kept an immaculate garden and had "never been sick a day in his life." My friend also said that his grandfather was a former enslaved person. The historical stories that are in this book happened in "the blink of an eye." This is not the time to suppress that history.

The journey of this church and racial autobiography has been interesting and fun but also has led me to a season of lamentation. However, that season has also shown glimpses of a humbler way to approach life with more empathy for others. I learned that I don't need to be a "Proud Texan." Instead, I need to be aware I am a Texan who is often blinded by pride.

"Humble yourselves before the Lord, and He will lift you up."

—James 4:10 NIV

Bibliography

Alwyn Barr. *Black Texans: A History of African Americans in Texas, 1528–1995*. Norman, Okla.: University of Oklahoma Press, 1996.

Alwyn Barr, and Antonio. *The African Texans*. College Station: Texas A&M University Press, 2004.

Atwood, James E., and Walter Brueggemann. *America and Its Guns: A Theological Exposé*. Eugene, Ore.: Cascade Books, 2012.

Bingham, Emily. *My Old Kentucky Home: The Astonishing Life and Reckoning of an Iconic American Song*. New York: Alfred A. Knopf, 2022.

Bonekemper, Edward H. *The Myth of the Lost Caus : Why the South Fought the Civil War and Why the North Won*. Washington, DC: Regnery Publishing, 2015.

Braithwaite, Barbara, ed. *A History of Richardson*, 1973.

Brown, Michael D. "Despite School Sentiment, Harding's Leader Said No to Integration." *Arkansas Times*, June 6, 2012.

Cash, W. J. *The Mind of the South*. New York: Vintage Books, 1991.

Church, Episcopal, and Oxford University Press. *The 1928 Book of Common Prayer*. Oxford University Press, USA, 2006.

Cone, James H. *The Cross and the Lynching Tree*. Maryknoll, New York: Orbis Books, 2011.

DiAngelo, Robin J. *White Fragility: Why It's so Hard for White People to Talk about Racism*. Boston: Beacon Press, 2018.

Elizabeth Madox Roberts, and M. E. Bradford. *The Great Meadow*. Rowman & Littlefield, 1992.

Equal Justice Initiative. *Lynching in America: Confronting the Legacy of Racial Terror*. Montgomery, Alabama: Equal Justice Initiative, 2017.

Foster, Douglas A. *A Life of Alexander Campbell*. Wm. B. Eerdmans Publishing, 2020.

Giant. DVD. Warner Brothers Entertainment, 1958.

Graff, Harvey J. *The Dallas Myth: The Making and Unmaking of an American City*. Minneapolis: University of Minnesota Press, 2008.

Hannah-Jones, Nikole, Mary N. Elliott, Jazmine Hughes, New York Times Company, and Smithsonian Institution. *The 1619 Project*. New York, N.Y.: New York Times, 2021.

Harding Alumni Magazine. "Administration Building to Be Named for Anthony Wright." March 2021. https://wordpress.harding.edu/harding/2021/03/23/administration-building-to-be-named-for-anthony-wright/.

Harrison, Lowell H. "Slavery in Kentucky: A Civil War Casualty." *The Kentucky Review* 5, no. 1, Article 4 (1983). https://uknowledge.uky.edu/kentucky-review/vol5/iss1/4.

Hazel, Michael V. *Dallas: A History of the Big "D."* Fred Rider Cotten Popular History Series, 1997.

Henry Morton Woodson. *Historical Genealogy of the Woodsons and Their Connections*. Memphis, Tenn.: Published by the Author, 1915.

History of Campbell County Tennessee. "Progenitor of Family Here Died in Indian Battle." https://www.tngenweb.org/campbell/hist-bogan/woodson.html.

Hoagland, Diane, ed. *Petit Jean 1969*. Harding College Press, 1969.

Hughes, Richard T. *Myths America Lives By: White Supremacy and the Stories That Give Us Meaning.* University of Illinois Press, 2018.

In the Heat of the Night. DVD. United Artists, 1967.

Isenberg, Nancy. *White Tras: The 400-Year Untold History of Class in America.* New York, New York: Penguin Books, 2017.

James Richard Rogers, and William Rogers. *The Cane Ridge Meeting-House.* The Standard Publishing Company, 1910.

James, Larry M. *The Wealth of the Poor: How Valuing Every Neighbor Restores Hope in Our Cities.* Abilene, Tex.: Abilene Christian University Press, 2013.

Kelley, Warren Ray. "The Restoration Movement's Attitude toward Slavery." Graduate School Thesis, 1974.

Key, Barclay. *Race and Restoration.* LSU Press, 2020.

Keyes, James. "Early Settlers of Greenup County, Ky.:Thomas B King. (Conclusion)." *Portsmouth Daily Times*, November 25, 1876.

Keyes, James. "Early Settlers of Greenup County, Ky.: Thomas B. King." *Portsmouth Daily Times*, November 18, 1876.

Kobes Du Mez, Kristin. *Jesus and John Wayne: How White Evangelicals Corrupted a Faith and Fractured a Nation.* New York, N.Y.: Liveright Publishing Corporation, , 2020.

L. Edward Hicks. *Sometimes in the Wrong, but Never in Doubt: George S. Benson and the Education of the New Religious Right.* Knoxville: University of Tennessee Press, 1994.

Lloyd Cline Sears. *For Freedom.* Sweet Publishing Company, 1969.

Lowell Hayes Harrison. *The Antislavery Movement in Kentucky.* University Press of Kentucky, 1978.

Manchester, William. *A World Lit Only by Fire: The Medieval Mind and the Renaissance: Portrait of an Age.* New York: Sterling Publishing Co., 2014.

Marion Brunson Lucas. *A History of Blacks in Kentucky: From Slavery to Segregation, 1760–1891*. Frankfort, K.Y.: Kentucky Historical Society, 2003.

Matthew Paul Turner. *Our Great Big American God*. Jericho Books, 2014.

McBrayer, Ronnie. *The Jesus Tribe*. Smyth & Helwys Publishing, 2011.

Meacham, Jon. *The Soul of America: The Battle for Our Better Angels*. New York: Random House, 2019.

Meade, Bishop. *Old Churches, Ministers and Families of Virginia (Volume II)*. Alpha Edition, 2021.

Moorehead, James Howell. "Religion in the Civil War: The Northern Perspective, the Nineteenth Century, Divining America: Religion in American History, TeacherServe, National Humanities Center." https://nationalhumanitiescenter.org/tserve/nineteen/nkeyinfo/cwnorth.htm.

Morrison, Latasha. *Be the Bridge: Pursuing God's Heart for Racial Reconciliation*. Colorado Springs, Colo.: Waterbrook, 2019.

Nina Mitchell Biggs, and Mabel Lee Mackoy. *History of Greenup County, Kentucky*. The Franklin Press, 1951.

Phillips, Michael. *White Metropolis*. University of Texas Press, 2010.

Reese, Jack Roger. *At the Blue Hole: Elegy for a Church on the Edge*. Grand Rapids, Mich.: William B. Eerdmans Publishing Company, 2021.

Robert Chao Romero, and Jeff M. Liou. *Christianity and Critical Race Theory*. Baker Academic, 2023.

Rupert Norval Richardson. *Texas*. Prentice-Hall, 1943.

Schutze, Jim. *The Accommodation: The Politics of Race in an American City*. Dallas, Tex.: Deep Vellum, La Reunion, 2021.

Scott, Madison. "George Benson's Name Remains on Auditorium." *The Bison*, September 4, 2020.

Seibert, Eric A. *Disarming the Church*. Wipf and Stock Publishers, 2018.

Stevenson, Bryan. *Just Mercy*. 2014. Reprint, New York: Delacorte Press, 2014.

The Dallas Daily Herald. "A Political Meeting in Dallas." June 13, 1860.

The Great Meadow. Metro-Goldwyn-Meyer, 1931.

Tisby, Jemar. *Color of Compromise: The Truth about the American Church's Complicity in Racism*. S.L.: Zondervan, 2020.

———. *How to Fight Racism: Courageous Christianity and the Journey toward Racial Justice*. Grand

To Kill a Mockingbird. DVD. Universal Pictures, 1962.

Wallis, Jim. *America's Original Sin: Racism, White Privilege, and the Bridge to a New America*. Grand Rapids, Mich.: Brazos Press, 2017.

Whitehead, Andrew L. *American Idolatry*. Baker Books, 2023.

Wood, Hannah. "Creating 'the 946:' the Provenance of a Harding History Display." *Tenor of Our Times:* Vol.10, Article 9 (April 29, 2021).

Zahnd, Brian. *When Everything's on Fire: Faith Forged from the Ashes*. Downers Grove, Ill.: Ivp, An Imprint Of Intervarsity Press, 2021.

Zahnd, Brian, and Walter Brueggemann. *Postcards from Babylon: The Church in American Exile*. Columbia, S.C.: Spello Press, 2019.

Notes

1   Barbara Braithwaite, ed., *A History of Richardson*, 1973.

2   Nina Mitchell Biggs and Mabel Lee Mackoy, *History of Greenup County, Kentucky* (The Franklin Press, 1951).

3   James Keyes, "Early Settlers of Greenup County, Ky -Thomas B. King," *Portsmouth Daily Times*, November 18, 1876.

4   James Keyes, "Early Settlers of Greenup County, Ky.-Thomas B King. (Conclusion)," *Portsmouth Daily Times*, November 25, 1876.

5   Nina Mitchell Biggs and Mabel Lee Mackoy, *History of Greenup County, Kentucky* (The Franklin Press, 1951).

6   Henry Morton Woodson, *Historical Genealogy of the Woodsons and Their Connections* (Memphis, Tenn.: Published By The Author, 1915).

7   History of Campbell County Tennessee, "Progenitor of Family Here Died in Indian Battle ," www.tngenweb.org, accessed November 1, 2023, https://www.tngenweb.org/campbell/hist-bogan/woodson.html.

8   Richard T Hughes, *MYTHS AMERICA LIVES by : White Supremacy and the Stories That Give Us Meaning.* (University of Illinois Press, 2018).

9   Nikole Hannah-Jones et al., *The 1619 Project* (New York, N.Y.: New York Times, 2021).

10 Nina Mitchell Biggs and Mabel Lee Mackoy, *History of Greenup County, Kentucky* (The Franklin Press, 1951).

11 *The Great Meadow* (Metro-Goldwyn-Meyer, 1931).

12 Alwyn Barr, *Black Texans : A History of African Americans in Texas, 1528-1995* (Norman, Okla.: University Of Oklahoma Press, 1996).

13 Lowell H. Harrison, "Slavery in Kentucky: A Civil War Casualty," *The Kentucky Review* 5, no. 1, Article 4 (1983), https://uknowledge.uky.edu/kentucky-review/vol5/iss1/4.

14 Marion Brunson Lucas, *A History of Blacks in Kentucky : From Slavery to Segregation, 1760-1891* (Frankfort: Kentucky Historical Society, 2003).

15 Emily Bingham, *My Old Kentucky Home : The Astonishing Life and Reckoning of an Iconic American Song* (New York: Alfred A. Knopf, 2022).

16 Jim Schutze, *The Accommodation : The Politics of Race in an American City* (Dallas, Texas: Deep Vellum, La Reunion, 2021).

17 Jack Roger Reese, *At the Blue Hole : Elegy for a Church on the Edge* (Grand Rapids, Michigan: William B. Eerdmans Publishing Company, 2021).

18 James Richard Rogers and William Rogers, *The Cane Ridge Meeting-House* (The Standard Publishing Company, 1910).

19 James Richard Rogers and William Rogers, *The Cane Ridge Meeting-House* (The Standard Publishing Company, 1910).

20 Douglas A Foster, *A Life of Alexander Campbell* (Wm. B. Eerdmans Publishing, 2020).

21 Warren Ray Kelley, "The Restoration Movement's Attitude toward Slavery" (Graduate School Thesis, 1974).

22 Latasha Morrison, *Be the Bridge : Pursuing God's Heart for Racial Reconciliation* (Colorado Springs: Waterbrook, 2019).

23 William Manchester, *A World Lit Only by Fire : The Medieval Mind and the Renaissance-Portrait of an Age* (New York: Sterling Publishing Co., Inc, 2014).

24 Latasha Morrison, *Be the Bridge : Pursuing God's Heart for Racial Reconciliation* (Colorado Springs: Waterbrook, 2019).,p78

25 Episcopal Church and Oxford University Press, *The 1928 Book of Common Prayer* (Oxford University Press, USA, 2006).,pg360

26 *Giant*, DVD (Warner Brothers Entertainment, 1958).

27 Jim Schutze, *The Accommodation : The Politics of Race in an American City* (Dallas, Texas: Deep Vellum, La Reunion, 2021).

28 Rupert Norval Richardson, *Texas* (Prentice-Hall, Inc., 1943).

29 Alwyn Barr, *Black Texans : A History of African Americans in Texas, 1528-1995* (Norman, Okla.: University Of Oklahoma Press, 1996).

30 Alwyn Barr and Antonio, *The African Texans* (College Station: Texas A & M University Press, 2004).

31 Michael Phillips, *White Metropolis* (University of Texas Press, 2010).

32 Jim Schutze, *The Accommodation : The Politics of Race in an American City* (Dallas, Texas: Deep Vellum, La Reunion, 2021).

33 Kristin Kobes Du Mez, *Jesus and John Wayne : How White Evangelicals Corrupted a Faith and Fractured a Nation* (New York, Ny: Liveright Publishing Corporation, A Division Of W.W. Norton & Company, Inc, 2020).

34 Jim Schutze, *The Accommodation : The Politics of Race in an American City* (Dallas, Texas: Deep Vellum, La Reunion, 2021).

35 Kristin Kobes Du Mez, *Jesus and John Wayne : How White Evangelicals Corrupted a Faith and Fractured a Nation* (New York, Ny: Liveright Publishing Corporation, A Division Of W.W. Norton & Company, Inc, 2020).

36 Larry M James, *The Wealth of the Poor : How Valuing Every Neighbor Restores Hope in Our Cities* (Abilene, Tex.: Abilene Christian University Press, 2013).

37 Hannah Wood, "Creating 'the 946:' the Provenance of a Harding History Display," *Tenor of Our Times:* Vol.10, Article 9 (April 29, 2021).

38 Hannah Wood, "Creating 'the 946:' the Provenance of a Harding History Display," *Tenor of Our Times:* Vol.10, Article 9 (April 29, 2021).

39 Barclay Key, *Race and Restoration* (LSU Press, 2020).

40 Lloyd Cline Sears, *For Freedom* (Sweet Publishing Company, 1969).

41 Lloyd Cline Sears, *For Freedom* (Sweet Publishing Company, 1969).

42 Barclay Key, *Race and Restoration* (LSU Press, 2020).

43 Barclay Key, *Race and Restoration* (LSU Press, 2020).

44 Madison Scott, "George Benson's Name Remains on Auditorium," *The Bison*, September 4, 2020.

45 "Administration Building to Be Named for Anthony Wright," *Hard-*

ing Alumni Magazine, March 2021, https://wordpress.harding.edu/harding/2021/03/23/administration-building-to-be-named-for-anthony-wright/.

46 Ronnie McBrayer, *The Jesus Tribe* (Smyth & Helwys Publishing, 2011).

47 Jon Meacham, *The Soul of America : The Battle for Our Better Angels* (New York: Random House, 2019).

48 Ronnie McBrayer, *The Jesus Tribe* (Smyth & Helwys Publishing, 2011).

49 Equal Justice Initiative, *Lynching in America : Confronting the Legacy of Racial Terror* (Montgomery, Alabama: Equal Justice Initiative, 2017).

50 Latasha Morrison, *Be the Bridge : Pursuing God's Heart for Racial Reconciliation* (Colorado Springs: Waterbrook, 2019).

51 Andrew L Whitehead, *American Idolatry* (Baker Books, 2023).